PROPHECIES

PROPHECIES

VISIONS OF THE WORLD'S FATE:
TRUTHS, POSSIBILITIES, OR FALLACIES?

HANS HOLZER

CONTEMPORARY
BOOKS
A TRIBUNE NEW MEDIA COMPANY

Library of Congress Cataloging-in-Publication Data

Holzer, Hans.
    Prophecies : visions of the world's fate : truths,
possibilities, or fallacies? / Hans Holzer.
       p.   cm.
    ISBN 0-8092-3473-4 (alk. paper)
    1. Prophecies (Occultism)   I. Title.
BF1791.H64   1995
133.3—dc20   95-32772
                                          CIP

Cover photo courtesy of National Aeronautics and Space
Administration

Published by Contemporary Books, Inc.
Two Prudential Plaza, Chicago, Illinois 60601-6790
Manufactured in the United States of America
International Standard Book Number: 0-8092-3473-4
10   9   8   7   6   5   4   3   2   1

Contents

Introduction

When it comes to opinions about the future of our world, people tend to fall into roughly three categories: those who really don't believe in any kind of prophecy or psychic predictions, those who are convinced that the dire predictions of the great prophets—from St. John to Nostradamus, from Malachy to Edgar Cayce—will come to pass exactly as they were made, and who live in a kind of undercurrent of fear of the future, and finally those who try to reasonably determine which predictions are likely to be borne out and which are not by examining the facts and the track record of the prophets.

I belong to the latter group, and thanks to my training and long experience as a professional parapsychologist, I can study prophecies dispassionately and rationally.

Over the years, I have learned that there is no such thing as 100 percent accuracy among those who attempt to predict the future. One might ascribe these inaccuracies to human imperfection. After all, psychics, mediums, and prophets are people, and the knowledge they impart must be filtered through their own imperfect (human) personalities and minds.

On the other hand, could it be the intent of the "system," or Divine Providence, to let us have just so much certainty and no more, and to give us foreknowledge only when it is proper for us to have it? I think so; it is a system that helps humanity along by hinting at what is yet to come, and still allows us our free will in how we choose to act upon the bits and pieces of advance knowledge we are given. Whatever we choose to call this—destiny, karma, free will—it is a very orderly and, I think, fair system: we cannot possibly "earn" good karma if we are not making decisions and choices and taking actions. The system provides us these opportunities, with encounters carefully programmed ahead of our becoming aware of them in the time stream, but the system also expects us to be individuals and express our will.

As I see it, yes, there is a destiny up ahead and it cannot be avoided. But destiny has its rules and laws, and within those we have a great deal of freedom of choice. How we choose will depend primarily on who we are as individuals in this lifetime and how we use our gifts, abilities, and talents, our senses of judgment and fairness, and our understanding of what is patently evil and what is obviously good.

Thus, while prophets can and do predict the coming of catastrophes of one kind or another, they cannot always predict our behavior when the event strikes. In addition, I think we have the power to change the course of future events once we understand their likelihood, and counteract their progression in ways that would balance impending negative forces with the power of the positive. We can effect such changes individually, and as part of groups and movements.

That there is another order among events than cause and effect was already clear to Carl Jung when he wrote of *acausal synchronicity*, or "the law of meaningful coincidence." This second order by which events may connect is seemingly in contradiction to cause and effect but is nevertheless just as scientific and well regulated as the more accepted order. Application of the law of acausal synchronicity to prophecy may account for some predictions but by no means for all of them. There is still the time gap.

Professor Gardner Murphy, one-time president of the American Society for Psychical Research and a psychiatrist at the Menninger Foundation, has published a comprehensive study of the question of retrocognition and precognition in which he states that both experiences are essentially alike— that both seeing ahead and seeing into an unknown past lift the percipient out of ordinary time.

Sixty-five years ago the noted English researcher J. W. Dunne published his "An Experiment with Time," in which he postulated that man sometimes has the ability to see a little around corners, so to speak, that he can actually extend his sense of time in the same way he can sometimes extend his five senses and have a sixth-sense experience. Dunne's thesis is, however, built on the assumption that these time extensions are primarily short.

This is not so in my view, as I will demonstrate when citing cases that have come to my attention.

To my mind there is no difference between prophecies or predictions that come true the next day and those that materialize ten years later. Both Dunne and Professor Murphy emphasize this subject, and their efforts are directed toward a better understanding of that faculty in man that makes prediction possible. This approach is necessary, of course, for man's faculties have been explored only to a very limited degree. But I find that the solution to the puzzle lies not only in the understanding and systematizing of man's paranormal abilities, but also in the understanding and grasping of the nature of time. Here is where we find a seemingly insurmountable obstacle to reason. How can an event, the components of which have perhaps not even been born or conceived, be clearly seen and experienced? A condition that has not yet come into existence has no optical or other sensory characteristics that an observer, human or machine, can study.

Logically, then, predictions are *impossible.* Thus we must seek an explanation in one of three areas outside logic.

1. The psychic person can somehow be projected ahead in time and can look at the event as if he were "outside" it.

2. The psychic looks at the person to whom the event will happen and can somehow interpret the future from that person's personal magnetic field.

3. The psychic gets a visual and informative message directly to his brain centers from a discarnate person (a "spirit"). This of course only shifts the emphasis to the spirit world. The discarnate, then, must be able to look ahead in time in order to communicate this information to the psychic.

In my opinion, all three theories lead to the same inescapable conclusion: No matter what the nature of time—even if it is nonexistent, objectively speaking, and merely a means of orientation for flesh-and-blood people—there is an order of things suggestive of prearrangement.

We know that the law of cause and effect is accepted universally, and that the second law, that of meaningful coincidence, is accepted by some researchers at least. Could there not be a third law governing relationships between all things, living beings and otherwise, a law based not on matter, on action of a material kind, or on coincidence and its variations, but on *attraction?*

As you sow, so you shall reap. Could it be that a spiritual-moral law governs the events that befall us? By exercising our free will to the extent we are capable of, utilizing our forces to do what is universally considered good, do we thus shape our destiny ourselves?

This would mean that the psychic person merely tunes in on a person's projected record, his "expectancy," so to speak. Whether the prophet sees or senses actual events projected for him ahead of the normal time stream or whether the events themselves are stationary, already existing "out there in time," and *man* is the moving object, eventually meeting up with his destiny when the particular crossroad in the time stream has been reached—either way, we are presupposing an orderly scheme of things somewhere beyond the physical. All religions have postulated the existence of a deity or deities capable of shaping man's fate. But it remains for parapsychology to prove such forces objectively.

Is our "number" completely determined at the time of birth, or even at conception, and are we merely acting out a master plan? Are we only puppets with a limited amount of free will to improve our grades? If so, for what? For the next incarnation? And who is in charge here? Who put him in charge? All these questions, hardly new to the philosopher and frightening in their implications to the empirical scientist, are central to the questions of prophecy and knowledge of future events.

After years of research and experimentation in the psychic field, and thousands of verified cases, I am convinced that an orderly system beyond the ordinary physical world does operate, a divine law to some, a natural law to others. I am certain that nothing in nature is pure chance or coincidence in the narrow sense of the word and that all events have meaning even beyond Jung's implications.

We are not pawns in a heavenly chess game, but we are part and parcel of the god force, whatever it may be, and have a more or less sharply defined destiny. I use the qualifying "more or less" because one of the contributing factors in our destiny seems to be our own deeds.

In the following pages I will demonstrate objective proof for my firm conviction.

PART I

Prophecies in Retrospect

CHAPTER 1

Prophecies Made by Professional Psychics

Sybil Leek, in addition to being one of the world's finest trance mediums, on occasion also made accurate predictions of a psychic nature.

On April 23, 1965, Sybil predicted a "complete upheaval of worldwide significance in the East to take place on October 16 [of 1965]."

Present when this statement was made were Sheila Rahter, vice president of the Brook Street Bureau of Mayfair, Ltd., a well-known employment agency, and several staff members of the Goodson-Todman Company, a television production firm, notably Frank Rather, an executive.

On October 15, one day ahead of the predicted date, Khrushchev was overthrown. Miss Rahter telephoned Sybil Leek to tell her that she was one day off with her prediction.

"No," Sybil said firmly, "this is not it. My prediction will come true tomorrow, the sixteenth."

And so it did. That was the day the Red Chinese exploded their first nuclear bomb, and the noise of it was indeed heard around the world.

On September 25, 1966, Sybil had a feeling that the United States would shortly experience a rash of unexplained fires. She felt this would occur from about November 12 onward and said so in the presence of two witnesses.

Chicago especially, she felt, would be in the headlines in this respect. On January 16, 1967, Chicago's huge new exposition hall, McCormick Place, burned down—cause unknown. The building was thought to have been highly fire resistant.

Betty Ritter was a highly respected medium and clairvoyant until the late 1970s. Most of her work dealt with personal predictions, but occasionally she foretold events of general significance, which is rather surprising, since Betty had no interest in politics or any detailed knowledge of world events beyond the average person's ability to read—and interpret—the newspapers.

On October 13, 1964, a man named Kenneth Kahn, of New York, visited Mrs. Ritter for a personal reading. Mr. Kahn was a union official by profession, and his interest in the occult was nothing more than a hobby. He had no forethoughts of what he wanted to hear from the medium, other than the vague, general hope of "getting something."

To his surprise, Betty Ritter insisted that his late mother was present and that she had a message for him. Expecting something personal, Mr. Kahn was further taken aback when the message was wholly political.

"Khrushchev will be falling down in two or three days" was how Betty Ritter interpreted the message from Kahn's mother.

At that time, the Russian premier's position was as firm as ever; no inkling of impending downfall had appeared anywhere in the world press. Mr. Kahn assured me that the last thing on his mind at that time was Khrushchev, so no one could accuse Betty of reading her sitter's mind.

On October 15, 1964, the ouster took place and caught the world by surprise. Mr. Kahn submitted a report of the prediction to the American Society for Psychical Research and commented:

> In their response, they seemed to find it strange that my mother would discuss a political matter with me. They not only seemed to find it strange—they seemed to find it suspicious.
>
> Yet there is nothing strange about it; it is quite simple. My mother and I had and have (I am a convinced believer in spiritualism) many interests in common—among which was politics.
>
> We often discussed politics and we both have decided and definite opinions about it. My mother, in the prediction, was reflecting and continuing that interest. Moreover, my mother had come from Russia as a small child and, naturally, anything relating to that country she would consider of interest. In addition, both my mother and myself opposed Communism or any other form of government that denied liberty and dignity to people.
>
> I must emphasize that my mother and I often discussed these matters. It seems to me the most natural thing that we should continue discussing subjects that we had always found absorbing.

On a subsequent occasion, Mr. Kahn again had a opportunity to test Betty Ritter's gift of prophecy, although the matter was not so far-reaching in its significance as the Russian premier's ouster.

Nevertheless, it affected some eight million people and as such certainly qualifies as a public event. Mr. Kahn has made the following statement about his experience with the medium, which clearly shows the presence of true precognitive powers in Mrs. Ritter.

June 15, 1966

To whom it may concern:

On January 3, January 10 and January 17, 1966, Mrs. Betty Ritter, in sittings held with me on those dates, made the following predictions in connection with the then current TWA strike and Mr. Michael Quill. I will enumerate them as to date and in the words written by Mrs. Ritter.

January 3, 1966—The settlement of the TWA [strike] is close. Maybe not this week. The rug will be pulled from under his [Quill's] feet. It may be a 40% increase in salary. Mr. Quill will be ill soon after this. A collapse—looks like a heart attack.

January 10, 1966—Strike should be over in three and a half hours or days. It will work out alright. The fare will stay.

January 17, 1966—Quill will not live long. He is sicker than people think.

A check of the newspaper stories of the times so indicated will readily show how closely the events followed Mrs. Ritter's predictions. Especially noteworthy is the prediction of Mr. Quill's illness and his subsequent passing away. It had been generally felt that the illness was merely a strategic device—a matter of tactics. Such, obviously, was not the case, as was shown.

It had also been felt that any strike settlement would immediately result in an increase of the prevailing fare. Here, too, flying in the face of public and expert opinion and very definitely putting herself on a limb, Mrs. Ritter's prediction has proved itself.

Kenneth W. Kahn

On February 28, 1967, Betty Ritter sent me a note, postmarked the same day, confirming what she had first told me on the telephone a week earlier. It was a firm prediction concerning future events that she wished to have recorded for the time when they would materialize.

"The war with North Vietnam will end sometime in May 1967, perhaps the 26th of May. It would be an American victory. China would enter the war to help North Vietnam. Also, I feel that Russia will take a hand in bringing about this peace. Only an escalation of war will bring this about."

The escalation coupled with peace-talk rumors is, of course, a matter of record.

Betty's note continued: "I also see a vision of Mao Tse-tung falling on the ground, meaning his end—an assassination."

Roberta Mueller is a professional astrologer living in Virginia Beach, Virginia. Astrologers do not predict the future; those who do are not using their astrological charts to do so, but rely on psychic interpretation. Astrology is merely a mathematical craft that can predict general trends in our lives but not actual events, since events and our reactions to them make up our individual fates, and astrology does not pretend to foretell individual fates. Miss Mueller contacted me on March 3, 1970, with a number of predictions that she said were based on her astrological charts. However, in interpreting these charts she quite obviously drew on some psychic reservoir within herself.

"The coming total solar eclipse of March 7, 1970, conjoins President Nixon's sun in his progressed chart. There could be some sort of plot uncovered concerning him. But the effect of the eclipse will last for weeks and even months thereafter, so I feel that Mr. Nixon's health may need care in the next few months; also he will be the scapegoat for conditions that are not entirely his fault." Mr. Nixon's escalation of the war in Cambodia certainly bore out this prediction, and the prediction clearly foreshadowed the Watergate scandal.

In early December of 1969, Miss Mueller told a newspaperman, Larry Bunko, of the Portsmouth, Virginia, *Star-Ledger*, that she foresaw machinery set up to reveal the status of American's foreign bank accounts. Several months later this actually took place. Congressional machinery was set in motion to force Americans with foreign accounts to reveal them. Also on December 30, in an interview she gave the *Star-Ledger*, Miss Mueller said. "The war in Vietnam will grind down after April." As of May 1970 there was a lessening of the conflict, although the war was still going on.

Miss Mueller also predicted another financial crisis, for November 1970. "The year's economic recession," she said, "will hardly slow inflation's upward spiral and unemployment. Welfare rolls will swell to an unprecedented degree."

As of May 1970 the U.S. unemployment percentage was higher than at any time since the days of widespread unemployment in the early days of Franklin D. Roosevelt's first term as president.

As far as the Middle East is concerned, Miss Mueller foresees "escalation of hostilities" and says it will all become steadily worse, climaxing in explosive violence.

Dave Hoy is a professional lecturer-mentalist who makes the college circuit regularly and with excellent success. He is an affable, friendly, well-educated man who has a long record of predictions that came true. According to the *Evansville Courier* of April 1, 1968, Hoy announced that President Lyndon Johnson would not seek reelection. This prediction was made January 1, 1967, well ahead of any period during which one might guess Johnson would seek no further tenure. The prediction was made in an article printed in the Sunday *Courier* and was one of eight predictions made at the same time, of which six came true. Other events Hoy has predicted include the Ohio River bridge disaster, which he foretold three months before the span collapsed.

June Weidemann was a nurse in the labor and delivery section of a hospital in a large city of Alabama. From the time she first became aware of her psychic abilities, she set aside two hours a day or more to devote to psychic research, with herself as the central rallying point. She decided to put some of her predictions into the form of a newsletter which she mailed to a limited number of people, both those interested in her work locally and scientists with interest in precognition. She called it *The Paranormal Research Bulletin,* and it appeared at irregular intervals from four to six times a year.

On February 1, 1957, she predicted and published in *The Paranormal Research Bulletin* that an overall depression would hit the entire country early in 1958. As a matter of fact, a recession started in December of 1957. On May 22, 1957, she predicted freak weather conditions causing blizzards in the Midwest. This occurred in December of the same year, crippling transportation over a wide area. On November 2, 1957, she predicted that Red China would turn against Russia in the near future. This, of course, is an established fact, although it happened several years after Mrs. Weidemann's prediction. At the time she made this prognostication, China and Russia were still good friends. On March 10, 1958, she predicted that we would see pictures of the planet Mars, taken by Americans, in our lifetime. This has already taken place. On September 5, 1958, she predicted a holy war in the area of Mecca during the next few months. This, she later felt, referred to the first Arab-Israeli conflict. On the same day she also predicted that there would be no full integration in the South for several years to come. As of the middle of 1970 the South had yet to integrate fully. On December 1, 1958, she predicted that some ICBM missiles would make history in the next year. This, she later felt, referred to the Cuban missile crisis. On April 13, 1959, she foresaw that Russia's leader would be purged within six months and disappear from the scene; and she also spoke of pending investigations of advertising claims of many prominent firms, with many products found harmful. This has occurred and is still occurring. On June 20, 1968, she made a number of predictions concerning that and the following year. The stock market would suffer in the late fall or the spring of 1969; we all know that it did. Race violence would reach its peak in the next two years and would then taper off, but scars would remain for many years.

On December 1, 1968, she had some additional predictions. Violent weather conditions would cripple New York and kill many people. A most unexpected heavy storm hit New York on February 8, 1969. Also on June 20, 1968, she predicted that Alaska would announce the discovery of a vital mineral in huge quantities. Years later, enormous new oil deposits were discovered under the Arctic wasteland of Alaska.

"The Vietnam War will peter out in two years," she said on June 20, 1968. "Troops will be withdrawn." As of May 1970 troops were being withdrawn as the war slowly became less virulent. Also on June 20, 1968, Mrs. Weidemann predicted, "The first space ship to the moon with men will bear American colors. A Soviet attempt will end in disaster." The Soviet space ship *Luna* crashed, and *Apollo 11* landed on the moon and returned safely.

Here are other predictions Mrs. Weidemann made concerning the future. She went on record with these statements on December 1, 1968. "I predict that China will try to take over Japan, her age-old rival, within the next few years." She also predicted some difficulty with the *Apollo 8* mission to the moon. As she saw it, in 1968, there seemed to be some worry when the vehicle did not appear from around the back side of the moon as quickly as it was supposed to. This worry would be short-lived, however, she said, for the vehicle would appear. This prediction may very well refer to the difficulty encountered by the *Apollo 13* mission, but perhaps it concerns a mission yet to come. Mrs. Weidemann predicted the return of Mau Mau raids, in Australia of all places, and that immigration will almost come to a halt from other countries there. She also predicted a slight shift in the poles of the earth, causing many weird weather conditions.

Under the dateline of September 15, 1969, June Weidemann had some additional predictions for the future. She foresaw peace in Vietnam by January of 1970, uneasy but permitting our troops to pull out. As of May 1970 there was no peace, but there was a kind of standoff, and troops were being pulled out slowly. There will be war in South America, probably Colombia. Riots will invade Vatican City and lay waste to treasures there. The world will see riots and unrest such as never seen before, and governments will be powerless to stop it. Thousands of people will be killed. This will bring a period of sanity and tight restrictions, which, however, will not last long—perhaps a year. These and other predictions remain to be fulfilled, however, and Mrs. June Weidemann has not always been correct. But she is a professional person with a good levelheaded personality, and her interest in the paranormal is purely scientific. In publishing or allowing me to use her personal predictions, she seeks no notoriety or financial gain.

Joseph de Louise was a hairdresser living in Chicago who became more and more interested in developing his psychic abilities and turned into a semiprofessional minor prophet. Mr. de Louise represents a typical American confronted with the evidence of his own psychic ability. I went to Chicago on April 27, 1968, and interviewed him in my suite at the Hotel Knickerbocker. Joseph de Louise looked like a good advertisement for his shop. He had bushy dark hair, a youthful appearance, and a lively way about him. There was nothing weird or fanatic about the way he described his psychic experiences. He was the father of six children, active in his community, and by and large a pretty average guy.

His first encounter with ESP came when he was only five years old; at the time his family lived in a small village in Sicily.

He told his mother he had seen his dead uncle and that in this vision his uncle had told him to dig in a certain spot on a farm; the place was called Giabellina. So the family went to that spot and started to dig. At first, nothing happened. But when they had dug six inches down, they came up with a little jewel box. In it was about three thousand dollars in cash. They never found out whether the money belonged to the uncle or to a stranger; they just used it. What made this early experience remarkable was not only the fact that the money was found, but also that little Joseph had described Uncle Pete in every detail, even though he had never met him.

When he was five and half years old, the family moved to America. At age eight the little boy kept seeing a certain lady in the neighborhood who had passed away some time before. She kept smiling at him out of what used to be her apartment on Cleveland Avenue on Chicago's North Side. His parents were then going through hard times, since it was the Depression, and the psychic talents of an eight-year-old could not be put to any practical use. The boy was sent to a Catholic school where the nuns tried to talk him out of any belief in psychic powers. He had completed the eighth grade when the navy called him; he was then only seventeen years old. He joined, serving in World War II. After the war he didn't do much of anything for a year or so, but he had had some psychic experiences while in the service. He had been in China, he had been in the Philippines, and his horizons had widened. In Shanghai he had met a local psychic who instructed him in developing his own psychic powers. He had always followed his own psychic consciousness. While stationed on Guam, one morning he and two other men were supposed to help unload some six-inch shells. He suddenly felt very ill and another man took his place. Some of the shells exploded, killing one of the men and hurting two of the others.

He decided to become a hairdresser. Gradually he found that he was telling his clients things about themselves and about their future. Word of mouth gave him the reputation of a neighborhood psychic, because many of the things he told his customers actually came true or were correct. But the first major event of his psychic career, so to speak, came when he predicted the bridge disaster on the Ohio River a year before it actually happened. This came about when he went on a radio program in Gary, Indiana, called *The Most Unusual People.* The program producer had found out about his gift of ESP, had been given a personal reading himself, and was impressed. What impressed the producer, Warren Frieberg, in particular, was the remark Mr. de Louise made concerning the producer's boss at the station. He told him that there was a horse the boss was interested in that should be checked out. When they did, they found that the horse had a bad leg. Since the producer's boss was about to buy the horse, he had time to change his mind. In gratitude, he sent Mr. de Louise a bouquet of flowers. By that time de Louise had purchased a large crystal ball to help him concentrate and conjure up visions rather than wait for them to come to him. He had been challenged by the radio producer to come up with some good predictions. He went home and looked in his crystal ball, and as he relaxed, he suddenly saw the vision of the Ohio River bridge. At the time he did not realize which bridge it was, but he described it in detail. He took the crystal ball with him to the station and again attempted to read it, and sure enough, the bridge appeared in his vision. As he was on the air, he spoke of a disaster that would happen very shortly involving this particular bridge. He said that it would cave in from the bottom because of weight problems. He described the cement giving in and said that this would be a large bridge, somewhere in the Midwest, going south from Gary, Indiana. To his horror, he also saw cars and people hanging from the bridge. He described all this to the amazed and perplexed radio people.

The Chicago Daily News of December 18, 1967, was filled with the account and photographs of the Ohio River bridge

disaster. It also contained a recapitulation of Mr. de Louise's
vision of the bridge disaster:

> On November 25, Joseph de Louise sat before a
> microphone at radio station wwca in Gary and said,
> "Before the end of the year a major bridge—not as
> large as the Brooklyn or Golden Gate bridges but a
> large one—will collapse, causing a great number of
> deaths and making newspaper headlines." Last Friday
> evening the Silver Bridge across the Ohio River at
> Point Pleasant, West Virginia, collapsed. The death toll
> is mounting. Joseph de Louise felt terrible about mak-
> ing the prediction, he said, but "I had to; I couldn't
> sleep." In his prediction he said the bridge tragedy
> would occur before the end of 1967, that it would be
> in a Midwestern state, and that it would be caused by
> the rotting away of piles holding the bridge or some-
> thing to do with the bottom of the structure, and that
> the large loss of life would make newspaper headlines
> across the country.

At the time this article was published in the newspaper, 16
bodies had been recovered; the search continued for dozens
more.

When he recovered from the shock of having made a major
prediction that had come true, Mr. de Louise turned to prophecy in a semiprofessional way. He started to make predictions
on a regular basis, sending copies of his prophecies to various
newspapers and scientific bodies interested in parapsychology.
He did not yet become a paid professional medium, and continued his readings for his customers and friends only. But a
local psychic society, called Psychic Science Research Foundation, headed by Grafton L. Beasley, took de Louise under its
wing and helped promote him to the outside world. His pre-

dictions did not come to him spontaneously for the most part. When someone asked him to make some prophecies—such as a newspaperman—he went home and concentrated and stared into his crystal ball. Then he came up with some vision, which he would in turn verbalize into actual predictions. When a reporter from the *Sun-Times*, Jerry Watson, asked him to make some predictions, he came up with "There will be no major riots this year in the United States, but an actual insurrection, which will take place probably in a Southern state. It will be bloody and put down by federal troops." This appeared in the *Sun-Times* under the dateline of January 8, 1968. On April 7, 1968, *The Chicago American* had the following report: "Lieutenant Governor Samuel H. Shapiro in a cable to President Johnson termed the riot 'insurrection.' Because of the Lt. Governor's telegram to Mr. Johnson, 5,000 federal troops were immediately flown to Chicago to put down the insurrection."

Of course, not all of Mr. de Louise's predictions came true, but the fact that more did than the law of averages would permit is amazing. Also in the *Sun-Times* of January 8, 1968, Mr. de Louise was quoted as predicting Ho Chi Minh would die shortly, which happened in 1969. Both the United States and Russia would suffer space disasters in 1968. (Russia certainly did, and the United States came close to one in 1970.) U.S. troops would be involved in other Asian wars. Mr. de Louise's psychic predictions for 1969—made during 1968—contain a number of statements that did not become reality, at least not in 1969. But there were several that bear reporting here. "I see a tragedy involving water around the Kennedys." This was long before the tragic drowning at the bridge in Massachusetts. "I see Mayor Daley and the chief of police making headlines in Washington when summoned concerning civil disorders." Both these men broke into national headlines in connection with the disorders during the Democratic convention in Chicago. "I see the arrest of over two hundred ringleaders of civil disorders, lessening the turmoil throughout the United States. This will follow after an attempt to burn several colleges."

The late Ethel Meyers worked with me primarily as a trance medium. Her clairvoyant powers became apparent almost from the beginning of her interest in psychic work.

Her first husband, Albert, died on July 7, 1944. On September 23 of that year, the first birthday he could not spend with her in the physical world, Ethel Meyers received an impulse to do some automatic writing, that is, writing controlled by someone in the so-called spirit world. True automatic writing is genuinely psychic in nature and must be distinguished from mere expressions of the medium's own unconscious.

After some personal expressions, which appeared in the handwriting of her late husband, Ethel asked him the question that was on everyone's mind: When will the war be over?

"May 8, 1945," Ethel's hand wrote, under Albert's control.

Ethel was doubtful. It was 1944; Germany lay defeated, and everyone thought it was all over but the shouting. But Albert's date was right, and the boys were not home for Christmas that year after all.

On June 5, 1953, Ethel asked Albert about the Korean War. Would there be a peace treaty signed soon?

In Albert's handwriting, Ethel wrote, "No peace treaty. A cease-fire July 27 of this year. I am looking ahead five years and I see no treaty of peace signed."

Ethel tore the page from her writing pad, gave it to her current husband, Daniel Meyers, to read and then deposited the sealed statement with *Daily News* lab technician Bernard Axelrod, a psychic researcher with whom both of us had worked in the past.

The date of the cease-fire was correct.

For two years, 1960 and 1961, I kept a record of the psychics who had read for me during that time. My purpose was not to tally what percentage of their predictions had become fact but to chart the regularity with which different psychics predicted the same events.

It stands to reason that if a statement is correct, more than one medium should be able to "get" its component facts. If a large number of receivers tune in a radio program at the same time, some will get the program and others will not; powerful receivers will get it clearly while others will get it less distinctly and some may not get it at all because of distance, malfunction, or atmospheric conditions.

I decided I would be satisfied if a portion of the psychics consulted by me came up with matching evidence.

Obviously, if only two mediums are used for a reading and both give different material, it cannot be said one is wrong and the other is right. They may both be right, or both wrong. But if half a dozen or more psychics read for the same person, there *should* be a certain percentage of matching or similar facts, even accounting for human failures and loss in transmission from *there* to *here*.

My method differs from pure laboratory experiments considerably because I go into the field for spontaneous phenomena—in this instance, readings by psychic persons of the same subject, me. But after I collect this spontaneous material, I analyze it according to orthodox statistical methods. This may not be the answer entirely, for statistics can mislead. Then again, a psychic reading is not the spontaneous phenomenon that a haunting or psychic manifestation is, since my requesting the reading introduces an element of experimentation. But the medium's lack of knowledge of my background and the irregularity with which I seek out these readings would bring it, in my opinion, within the framework of what is generally called spontaneous phenomena in parapsychology.

I should like to point out that the often-mentioned theory of mind reading, or the tapping of the subject's conscious and unconscious mind by the reader, deserves some healthy skepticism. For one thing, no one has ever proved conclusively that one person can really read the mind of another. Telepathy exists, but only between two individuals well attuned to each other. The readings given by a medium to a stranger cannot be explained by telepathy.

If I were to confront a psychic reader while having well-defined thoughts of names and facts, perhaps the reader could pick up the trend of my thoughts. But to believe that the reader can dig out of the unconscious mind names and facts long forgotten or submerged seems to me rather far-fetched, and a disservice to the amazing ability of some good psychics to come up with pertinent material. Added to this must be the many instances in which the unconscious mind did not yet have the information and thus could not have been the source.

I do, however, think that a person is surrounded by a magnetic field that extends beyond his physical body, and that this field contains certain impulses pertaining to both past and future. It may be that some of these impulses contribute to the knowledge gained by a psychic reader, but there are many cases where other explanations are on the whole more logical and preferable. Some mediums will tell the subject that their information is given them by discarnates, relatives, controls, or others and that they are merely the channels through which the information flows. This, of course, relieves them of responsibility for the truth of the material. Others make no such claim but ascribe it to their own ESP talents.

It is a moot point whether the medium is self-made or helped by unseen hands from beyond the veil; mediumship still involves psychic talents and the ability to obtain information through methods other than the five senses.

To the reincarnation theorist this presents no problem: at birth, we are given a sort of ID card—an identity stamp already containing our life pattern from beginning to end. We ourselves may not be privileged to read it, but the psychic person can interpret it for our benefit.

Some of these "life readings" are enormous frauds, usually the work of imitators of the great psychic Edgar Cayce. But there are also many genuine readings of future events by honest mediums who simply sense these events in a kind of visionary flash. I have always felt that the portion having to do with future events tends to be genuine and is certainly capable of verification, while the previous incarnations tend to be fanciful and rarely borne out by proof.

I am still seeking a "life reading" medium who can give a subject a list of his past incarnations and have them verified scientifically as to names, dates, and circumstances. No doubt such cases exist, but are submerged and waiting to be discovered amid the waves of fakery.

To get back to my statistical chart, undertaken for the years 1960 and 1961, here are the results:

> *Number of psychics consulted:* Six
> *Total number of consultations:* Ten
> *Sex of psychics consulted:* Female
> *Age group:* Middle-aged and older
> *Health:* Good

Recurrence of certain letters or words

> *J:* Five times
> *F, M:* Four times
> *A, G, Doctor, John, W:* Three times
> *Max, Robert, H, E, B, William, George, Elizabeth, Grace, Charles, R, Virginia, S, Harry:* Twice
> *Other:* Once

Matching predictions:

> *Max:* Carolyn Chapman, November 3, 1960; Betty Ritter, July 18, 1960
> *Robert:* Carolyn Chapman, November 3, 1960; Betty Ritter, October 4, 1960

Doctor: "Titan," February 27, 1960; Betty Ritter,
     July 18, 1960, and October 4, 1960
R: "Jesse," January 26, 1961; Betty Ritter, July 18,
     1960; Laurette, May 21, 1957 (brought in here
     to compare with earlier data)
M: "Jesse," January 26, 1961; "Titan," February 27,
     1960; Betty Ritter, July 18, 1960; Laurette, July
     7, 1960

These examples will suffice to make my point, namely, that correspondences do occur; they are more frequent when the prediction is comparatively simple, such as a single letter, and less frequent when an entire word is involved. The psychics tested did not know each other even by reputation.

Consistency of Predictions by the Same Psychic

Genuine mediums will be consistent without even trying. A professional reader who sees hundreds of people every month cannot possibly keep mental track of every detail of the readings. The fakers keep index card files, such as were discovered in some of the American Spiritualist camps a few years ago, and exchange information on "steady" customers.

I have never seen a medium take notes while reading for me. Betty Ritter wrote down letters and words impressed upon her and handed me the notes at the end of the session. She was the only psychic I knew who used pencil and paper. I would not permit the taking of notes by anyone but myself. There is no way a genuine psychic can make a record of his or her reading. I am alert to such devices as tape recorders and have never found evidence that one was used in my presence.

Thus, it boils down to this: if a medium is consistent over a long period of time, and if this consistency covers a number of instances not easily remembered, it must be assumed that the medium is giving an authentic reading in each instance, and that the source of this paranormal information, whatever it may be, is repeating the material because it is still correct!

Genuine mediums will not predict exact time; in fact, they will freely admit that telling events beforehand is far easier than pinning them down to a date, because in the psychic world, time as we know it does not exist. Thus, a prediction may take some earth time to materialize. The psychic, or another psychic perhaps, may give the same prediction again, since the time for its fulfillment has not yet arrived.

The impatient may find this hard to take, but the fact is that eventually an impressive number of predictions made to me *have come true.* Sometimes, especially when pressed, a medium will give a wrong date, but the event depicted does otherwise occur as described. This has happened to me in a number of instances and proves, to me at least, that the time element cannot be quite what we think it is, that there is a trickiness to time we are not yet fully cognizant of, that perhaps emotional and developmental factors have some influence on the timing of events—time being no absolute dimension, but a secondary factor depending on both immaterial and personal influences.

Betty Ritter was the most consistent medium I've known. Some of the names or initials she saw connected with my life were in her readings for several years. Some have already become of significance in the material world; some have yet to be.

An important point to remember is that certain elements of chance must be considered. Thus, if a reader says you will have some business with a John or a Charles, chances are that you will, because of the great number of people named

John or Charles in this world and the probability that somehow, somewhere, you will have some sort of dealings with one
of them. It is only when the predicted material becomes
specific by being narrowed down either in time, space, or
circumstances, that we consider the paranormal element
as likely.

Chapter 2

Amateur Prophets: How Accurate Are Their Predictions?

Whereas I have dealt with professionals in the psychic field making predictions of a prophetic nature in the previous chapter, I am reporting here the statements of average people who are not professional psychics or prophets in any sense. Nevertheless, the quality of their visions, impressions, or dreams does not differ in quality or accuracy from that of those who make their living working in the psychic field.

I deal here with prophecies made between late 1960 and early 1970. Only by examining prophetic statements made a number of years ago in the light of what we know as truth today, in the '90s, can we gain an understanding of the nature of prophecy itself, at least to the extent that it applies to these average individuals. The truly rare great prophets will be dealt with in a later chapter, with appropriate evaluations.

There must be thousands of people all over the world who at one time or other feel impelled to make predictions. Most of these predictions are about friends, neighbors, family. When they come true, those who make them may be amazed, or they may take them in their stride. Once in a while these predictions have to do with famous people or world events. When such predictions become reality, there is always a question involved: Did the person really have a psychic premonition, or was he drawing simply on well-known facts about the celebrity or event? But, allowing for a certain percentage of such explanations, there still remain a good number of people in all walks of life capable of foreseeing, at odd times, events still in the future.

There is no doubt that some people with very little knowledge of world events or very little education have, from time to time, come up with precise predictions that would require intimate knowledge of the situation or personalities involved if these predictions were based on empirical knowledge and not on psychic material. I am satisfied that many of these people do not in fact possess such empirical training, but are able to foretell future events or events pertaining to people in the public eye not from some acquired knowledge about them, but from something within themselves on a very deep level of consciousness.

In this chapter I am dealing with the "civilians" among those who make psychic predictions. None of these people has seen fit to engage in public readings or to start on a career as a professional medium. They are happy being businessmen, housewives, teachers, doctors, and workers, and they have on the whole accepted their psychic abilities as part of their personalities. They are not future minor or major prophets, but simply people who have been able to tune in on the future, for reasons none of us really knows. It is still a great mystery to me why some people are chosen to become prophets while others are not—why some people who are not particularly well suited to be spokesmen for humanity do in fact become spokesmen because of their gifts, while others seemingly very qualified do not have the advantage of psychic vision. But, then, I have not yet thrust into the inner workings of fate itself. All I and others who work in this field realize is that there is a divine order of things—or perhaps a supreme law—that has so ordained and that keeps things going in a way that seems to suit the law and not necessarily us. All we can do on this side of the curtain is study the effect the law has upon us and learn more about ourselves, especially when we are channels for the knowledge coming from the other side.

Most if not all of the people reporting paranormal incidents of a prophetic nature to me over the years have had other ESP experiences all through their lives. Sometimes these were very minor—such as knowing when the telephone would ring or when a certain person would call for a visit. At other times these incidents involved seeing a deceased person, or foreknowledge of impending death, or perhaps accidents that occurred as foreseen or, in other cases, that could be forestalled because of the warning received. But there is always a history of some sort of prophecy prior to the incident. I know of no case where a person experiences a prophetic vision and never has another in his lifetime. Those who may think that a certain incident is unique in their lives and that it has never occurred before nor will occur again may be simply disregarding minor incidents of the same general nature. ESP talents develop over a period of time—sometimes slower, sometimes quicker. In going over one's earlier experience, one can easily spot some incidents that would fall into this category.

Pauline Graff lived in western New York State. On December 9, 1968, she reported two precognitive dreams to me. The first of the two dreams occurred to her the night of November 22, 1968. It had something to do with Senator Barry Goldwater and a legal matter. She saw him refusing to sign some paper until the legal rights were understood; she said there was a big hassle about signing the paper and that he was right. It was in early 1970 that Senator Goldwater won a libel suit and signed documents to end it. The second dream Mrs. Graff reported to me occurred on December 7, 1968, at 6:18 A.M. She awoke startled and rather sad. She had just witnessed, in the dream state, an American rocket going right to left over a body of water and exploding; and she saw herself run out of the house to watch the sky. It was low enough to see the shape of it and the lights going on and off. Suddenly it blew up in a fiery ball of flame. Silently she asked why, in the dream, and received a reply that "it must have been over some water." Her own interpretation of this prophetic dream was that one of our next rockets would develop some kind of electrical problem with the lights going on and off and that it would suddenly explode, possibly as it was landing in the ocean.

Mrs. Mary Nelson lives in a small community in southern California. She has no background in psychic phenomena, very little education, and no contact at all with the literature in the field. But certain things have happened in her life that have puzzled her for a long time. When she was only ten years old, she told a newly widowed aunt that she would remarry, be proposed to on water, and honeymoon with ducks flying overhead. The aunt was proposed to on a ship and honeymooned in Alaska. Mrs. Nelson began to read people's palms, but instead of concentrating on the lines in the hands, she saw pictures coming up before her inner eye. Much of what she told her friends came true. Eventually she was compelled to write down predictions for the coming year as the old year drew to a close. On July 22, 1969, she put down some of her predictions for the immediate future. These included a flood in her area of California, the return of Victorian fashions, and an earthquake in South America. She also saw an African leader assassinated with someone with a red and gold hat concerned. This latter statement interested me most of all her predictions, because Tom Mboya was assassinated sometime after the prediction was made, and the president of his country, who was indeed most concerned, does wear a red and gold hat on formal occasions.

I often wonder why important people or leaders of one kind or another, in various fields, attract so many predictions. The easy answer would be that people know more about them than about average people; but I suspect it has to do with their magnetism, with the amount of power within their personalities that is somehow stronger than the power contained in the bodies and personalities of average people. Could it then be that, because of this excess energy streaming out from the people in the limelight, sensitive people get images pertaining to their future? Is it perhaps because of the stronger magnetic field, the stronger auric impression that these people project, that so many people who don't even know them personally receive impressions about them pertaining to the future?

Audrey White Wiley is a housewife in Kentucky. She lives in an upper-middle-class neighborhood; her husband works for an industrial company and she has two little girls. She has no particular interest in the paranormal, but one incident did disturb her to the point of contacting me. One September day in 1969 Mrs. Wiley and two neighborhood friends were having coffee. Their conversation somehow turned to the popular television personality Art Linkletter. One of the young women asked, "Isn't it a shame about Art Linkletter's child committing suicide?" Mrs. Wiley replied that she had heard nothing about it and that it must have happened while she was away in Europe, during June. No more was said about it. Imagine her shock when Art Linkletter's daughter did kill herself in October of the same year. Naturally she contacted her two friends immediately to discuss this terrible event. But to her amazement, Mary, the neighbor whom she had heard ask the question, did not recall having said it. None of those present remembered the question having been asked. This puzzled Mrs. Wiley even more. Did she dream the whole thing? If so, why, since there had never been any connection between herself and Art Linkletter's daughter? If the question was not asked by Mary, and Mrs. Wiley heard it being asked with her inner ear—psychically, that is—this would also constitute an extrasensory experience. It makes very little difference whether the question was actually spoken aloud or she was merely impressed with it; the fact that she had this knowledge long before the event took place is the paranormal element. Mrs. Wiley says she remembers no particular psychic experiences either before or after this incident, except for minor déjà vu experiences. But that event led her to become interested in extrasensory perception.

Sometimes receiving premonitory material involves personal feelings, and I am not always sure whether I should suppress material that might hurt someone's feelings or let it go through. A case in point involves the late television and radio personality Joe Pyne. I first met Mr. Pyne on his own program, when he interviewed me in rather a rough manner. Mr. Pyne quite obviously was not a believer in the psychic element in man. He was an able and hard-hitting commentator and interviewer, and he thought he was doing the world a service by attacking and often destroying the arguments of those who believe in the supernatural. Many of Mr. Pyne's guests deserved to be attacked, to be sure—but many more did not. Frequently he would use rather rough and insulting tactics to rattle his guests, who in turn would be less than successful in putting forward their point of view. He tried the same with me but found that I could use his language, too. Consequently our interview turned into a verbal battle, at the end of which Mr. Pyne shrugged his shoulders, held up my then-current book and nodded good-bye.

Subsequent interviews on his program were far more congenial. Joe Pyne was quick in learning a lesson. He realized that I would not let him get away with any adverse statements about psychic matters or myself, and, as a consequence, we got along quite well in later periods. As a matter of fact, my last appearance on his program, toward the end of 1968, found us almost chums. I had written a book called *Star in the East*, dealing with Biblical verification. Mr. Pyne seemed particularly interested in the question of whether there was a hereafter, scientifically speaking.

It was about that time that I learned that he had a fatal disease and that his time was limited. As his disease progressed, his interest in psychic matters seemed to have become somewhat less academic. But he never discussed either this or his illness with anyone. Joe Pyne was a strong man who believed to the end that his illness was his own private affair. I learned about it in a strange way.

On December 5, 1968, I received a letter from Mrs. Mary Shewell, who lived in a small town in southern California. She had had ESP experiences on and off for many years. On one occasion she had a dream in which she saw Satan, who had been turned loose, and a woman with red hair. She told this dream to her husband the next morning, feeling very foolish about the whole thing. When she picked up the newspaper that morning, she found on the front page an article telling of a sexual deviant who called himself Satan, having committed another murder the night before; the victim was a redheaded girl from Ohio. But the dream vision that disturbed her on this December day in 1968 and which compelled her to contact me was something else. She told me, "Here is another dream that hasn't come true but has bothered me quite a bit as it seemed so vivid. On October 18, 1968, at 4:30 A.M., I dreamed I was watching the *Joe Pyne Show* on TV. He seemed very sentimental. He was wearing a dark suit. At the last part of his show he said, 'Ladies and gentlemen, when I leave here I go directly to the hospital for a serious operation.' He mentioned his illness, which I can't remember now. He said things like, 'Whatever will be, will be.' There were tears in his eyes. Later my husband came in and said, 'I just heard, Joe Pyne is

dead.' I turned on KLAC. Someone was saying, 'We are all crying here at the sudden and terrible news of Joe Pyne's death.' "
Mary Shewell wondered what would make her have a dream like that. She, of course—along with the public in general—had no inkling of Joe Pyne's fatal illness. It was only a short time before his actual death that any news of it leaked out, since broadcasting circles do not like to divulge this sort of information about their stars. During 1968 and 1969 only his close family and a few people in the broadcasting industry knew about his problem.

I deliberated for a while what to do about this letter. I held no love for Mr. Pyne, nor did I have any hatred for him. As a matter of fact, I had a great deal of compassion for him. After some weeks of hesitating, I sent a copy of the letter to his producer, Hal Peretz, with the request to do with it what he saw fit. When I met Hal a little later in Los Angeles again, he told me that he had kept the letter in his files but had not shown it to or discussed it with Mr. Pyne. Even Pyne's own producer was not permitted that sort of intimacy.

This vision came to Mrs. Shewell on October 18, 1968. In November of 1969 Pyne gave up his television show. A spokesman for the station then announced that he was withdrawing due to illness. On January 21, 1970, he underwent surgery for removal of a lung, since he suffered from lung cancer. Then, on March 23, 1970, he died at Cedars of Lebanon Hospital in Los Angeles. Mary Shewell had apparently foreseen both Pyne's farewell broadcast and subsequent death at the hospital. She could not have guessed it, since knowledge of his illness was not available to her either at the time of the psychic vision or for a considerable time afterward. In the dream, the time element seems to be condensed, as often happens, since the dream state eliminates conventional time and space ideas. Thus, the farewell television appearance and the announcement of Joe Pyne's death are put side by side, when in actuality they were separated by several months. What must be emphasized again is that in October of 1968 the death of Joe Pyne at the age of forty-four was an improbable guess.

A housewife named Eve Frey, of Fort Bragg, California, has had a lifetime of psychic experiences, many of them attested to by neighbors or friends. But her ESP incidents and her experiences with hauntings do not interest me in this context; her predictions, however, do. In this connection, it is of interest that on July 8, 1968, she had a waking vision as she was resting quietly in her home. She saw a military leader being buried near a small white building, surrounded by rich, grassy earth. As she was wondering why there was so little ceremony to it, she saw the man's name flashed before her eyes—but the only thing she could grasp was the initial *E*. Months later, when President Eisenhower died, she saw the funeral on television. Instantly she recognized the spot she had seen in her vision many months before.

Yossedel M. Desta was an Ethiopian student studying psychology in San Francisco. Paranormal incidents had occurred to him from time to time. The one he found particularly engrossing, however, occurred to him in the summer of 1969, during one of his frequent naps. He is still not sure whether it was a dream or a vision, but he seemed to be present at two very real incidents. Apparently Mr. Desta witnessed guerrilla warfare in the cities of America. One place was the familiar Market Street near Powell Street in San Francisco, where people board cable cars. Gunfire was exchanged by soldiers in army clothes. It was hard to distinguish who was who. People in the streets were forced to lie down. Hippies and priests and nuns tried to intervene with flowers. Then the scene faded from his inner screen. The second vision concerned the emperor of Ethiopia, Haile Selassie. Mr. Desta saw his emperor assassinated and dying from bullet wounds. The place Desta described is close to Union Square, where political demonstrations take place from time to time. What makes Mr. Desta's description interesting is the fact that he felt that he was present when these events took place, looking down upon the scene, as it were, and he had difficulty accepting them as dreams. Selassie was, in fact, killed in 1975. Many believe the emperor was assassinated.

I can easily believe that in less enlightened times people accepted the idea of hereditary witchcraft and persecuted people for the simple fact that they were born with second sight and were the children of people with second sight. There is such a thing as hereditary witchcraft, but it means simply belonging to a family practicing the "old religion" for many generations past. However, frequently extrasensory perception runs in the family, generally on the mother's side. It can be inherited and can be passed on, although there seems to be no way of controlling it. Wishful thinking will not make it so. On the other hand, suppressing this talent will not really impede it. I am thinking of this as I consider the case of Earl Lane, a resident of North Carolina. The reason he contacted me was not to discuss his own amazing experiences with ESP, but to ask for counsel concerning his son, who had also developed this ability. The ironic part is that the son had kept his ESP experiences from the father, and the father from the son. Finally, after almost twenty years, they managed to talk to each other about it. But, since the son had recently married a girl of foreign extraction who spoke very little English, the father was justly concerned that the young bride might become even more confused by the knowledge that her husband possessed psychic power. Both father and son had for years received what they called "calamity material"—that is, hints of future catastrophes. They were not exactly elated by this talent; neither did they panic. The son was an air force sergeant and had to be careful about such matters. The father, however was retired and engaged in building activities; at one time he was an officer in the United States Merchant Marine. His mother also had ESP.

In the farm area in which Earl Lane had grown up, his mother was known to be possessed of second sight. Earl Lane first noticed his unusual ability when he was a teenager. On one occasion, his eldest brother, Gurney, had hauled some tobacco to market about twenty-five miles from their home. While he was still at the market and young Earl was sorting some more tobacco in their barn, he suddenly saw his brother's bill of sale in detail. He didn't dare mention it to anyone, or he might have been slapped for foolishness. But when his brother arrived and before anyone else had spoken, Earl quoted him the exact amount of the sale and startled him with it. The brother admitted that no one had seen that bill except himself.

Mr. Lane had a particular talent for visions concerning future developments of mankind, as well as tragedies. Many years before there was such a thing as a jet airplane engine, he had a vision of such an engine. This picture shook him up so badly he went to see a local doctor in his hometown. This doctor, by the name of Stricklin, was very kind to him, but after the young man had explained how this engine without a crankshaft would run without pistons and without any propeller, the doctor gently told the young man that this was merely a fantasy and to forget it. From that moment on young Mr. Lane was more careful about whom he would confide his visions to. A little later he had a vision of a delta-wing aircraft flying out of the east of China and out over the sea. It was many years later before such a plane was developed. In 1950 he was sailing through the Philippine Sea, and aboard ship there arose an argument concerning the Near East. The wireless officer and the third engineer discussed Israel and asserted that the little country would certainly be overrun and couldn't last much longer. At this moment Mr. Lane heard himself say, "But, gentlemen, on the contrary, Israel will become much larger and there will be Israeli troops walking along the Suez Canal, and all her borders will change." Everybody laughed at such a remark, but it all came to pass, as everyone knows. At the same time, in 1950, Mr. Lane also predicted that Russia and China would go to war against each other. That, too received nothing but sneers.

Mrs. Anne D. was employed by the Virgin Islands government on Saint Thomas. From time to time she had specific visions, usually while awake, of world events. These visions naturally concerned her. She contacted me after she had read one of my books. Some of her visions were quite interesting. On February 11, 1969, she had a waking vision in which she saw the Eiffel Tower in a state of collapse. Behind it she saw a brilliant sun rising. Her own interpretation of this vision was that the government of France would fall and a new kind of France would emerge afterward. More frightening is a vision she had on January 26, 1969:

> In a vision I saw a beautiful city, gleaming white, built on a plateau-like wall. Everything was white—all the buildings, the walls on which the city stood. The buildings were of ancient origin and there were temples and mosques among them. As I gazed at the scene, I could see a rough formation to my left, and two men dressed in Arab-style clothing were shading their eyes with their right hands while they looked across a chasm or separation at the city in the distance. They were kind of leaning over so they could see better. I saw a huge white mist descend and cover the entire city; then a red glow seemed to rise in a cloud until the entire city was enveloped, and the glow rose toward the sky and the top was sort of flat and dark around the edges. Then it slowly descended, and when everything had cleared away, the city had vanished. Where it once had

stood was nothing but embers. I believe that I saw the destruction of Jerusalem.

Now, one could say that the facts of the existing Arab-Israeli conflict might have produced such a vision in the unconscious mind of Mrs. D. After all, the possibility of destructive warfare involving Jerusalem is present as long as the tension in the Middle East exists.

What makes this vision, however, more interesting—or should I say, frightening—is another vision that occurred to Mrs. D.:

In late February of 1968, I dreamed that a vessel resembling a frigate and having many sails anchored off the coast of the island of Anguilla. It was night, about 2:30 A.M., but I could see the lowering of long, funny-looking rowboats, propelled by oarsmen. There were armed men also in these boats; they were wearing uniforms which were strange to me, and these were topped with French-style berets. When the rowboats came to a short distance offshore, I saw the men armed with rifles, on which bayonets were mounted, get quietly out of the boats and wade ashore. They carried their weapons over their heads, so that they wouldn't get wet. On reaching the shore of a sleeping town, the men carried their weapons at the ready position, with their left hand cupping the barrel and right hand on the trigger. The landing was accomplished without incident, but on their reaching the town, the citizens began to awaken to find themselves invaded, and a scuffle ensued in which several persons were hurt. At this point I woke up. Since at that time there had been talk of St. Kitts' invading Anguilla, I told several natives of the island of Anguilla about my dream. Most of them laughed at me, especially when

I informed them that the "invaders" had all been white men. I jokingly told them that it looked as if the French would take over the island. But to Mr. Hugh O., a fellow government employee, I transmitted my fear that real danger of invasion existed. I couldn't tell him how soon; all I could tell him was that it was going to happen. On March 14, on my way to Puerto Rico, I met another resident of the island by the name of Dorothy L. I told her that the rumored invasion of Anguilla would actually occur within the next few days. On March 17, 1969, I called Hugh O. and told him that the time for my dream to come true was at hand. Again I told him my dream in detail and mentioned my fears for the safety of the residents of the tiny island. He later told me that, in view of my great concern, he called a conference with his brothers, and those who had wives and children booked passage and went home to Anguilla. My husband is not a believer in psychic matters, but whether he wanted to hear it or not, I informed him on the night of March 18, 1969, that "during the night, between 2:00 A.M. and 5:30 A.M., the British will have taken over Anguilla."

It is, of course, a historical fact that her dream came true that night in every detail, just as she had foreseen it. The frustrations of having visions in great detail and not being able to prevent tragedy lay heavily upon Mrs. D.'s shoulders. But even if she could get through to higher government sources and be accepted as a true clairvoyant—which indeed she was—what could be done to prevent such tragedies? How could one even begin to interfere with the course of nature, or with history, in order to forestall that which had not yet come into being? The entire question of destiny, free will, and the nature of time is involved in such a problem.

In October and November of 1968, Mrs. D. had recurrent dreams of an airplane crash. The first two dreams were about a month apart. She would awaken at the moment of the crash. But the third time it was an even worse nightmare. She saw a small twin-engine plane crash into a two-story house on a hillside in the vicinity of Frenchtown on the island of St. Thomas. She clearly saw the plane burst into flames as it crashed onto the roof of the building. Then she saw a group of young men climb into the plane from on top of the building. They went down into the inferno and started to carry out bodies that were burned black. They laid them down a distance away from the crash, and she could see many persons rushing back and forth and the fire department vehicles as they arrived. Upon awakening from this nightmare, she was very nervous, and she was equally positive that the dream would eventually come true. She told anyone who would listen, but all her friends thought that she was slightly deranged and paid no attention. The vision came true in almost every detail about a month later. A twin-engine aircraft crashed into a two-story building, killing several of the building's occupants and some of the plane's passengers.

Elaine Morganelli is a California housewife who has had psychic experiences most of her life. Many of her predictions to friends and neighbors have come true. While she is a devout Christian, she has frequent communications with discarnate spirits and reports on these encounters in great detail during her contacts with me. In addition to her mediumship, however, she has made certain predictions that are vouched for by competent witnesses. For instance, she predicted in May of 1967, in a letter mailed to her brother, Lewis Olson, also of California, that "on June 4 there will be a presidential assassination." She assumed this dealt with President Lyndon Johnson; it turned out that Robert Kennedy, a presidential candidate, was assassinated June 4, 1968. On June 9, 1968, she mailed a letter to the secretary of the navy containing the statement, "You will find the submarine *Scorpion* at the bottom of the sea twenty miles west of the Azores." This was confirmed later. On

August 7, 1968, she made the following prediction to the American Society for Psychical Research: "The Czechs will swallow Russia's will. The *Pueblo* crew will be flown back to the United States. Abe Fortas will be out on his ear. There will be an outbreak of armed conflict in the Sudan, with blood flowing in the streets in the near future." All of these predictions came true. In the spring of 1968 she dreamed that Richard Nixon was standing with his wife and daughters in front of a microphone, smiling from ear to ear, waving to a huge crowd, while an announcer shouted, "A landslide victory for Richard M. Nixon!" Her prediction appeared in *The Los Angeles Herald Examiner* under the heading, "Seers Peer at Politics." In the spring of 1968 Mr. Nixon's victory was by no means certain. On August 10, 1969, Morganell wrote down a prediction concerning Bishop James Pike and mailed it to a friend, Arthur Charles, of Hollywood, California. The prediction read, "Extend the light also to Bishop James A. Pike, who is in grave danger and totally unprepared for his soon-to-be-realized fall." Bishop Pike's body was discovered September 7, 1969, in Judaea.

Paul Gagnon is an artist who has lived both in the United States and abroad. On December 18, 1967, he had a vision involving impending disaster with Asians; somehow he felt danger from those quarters. At the same time he had an impression that President Johnson would quit and Nixon would take over the presidency.

Elaine Jones is a housewife living in San Francisco, California. She has read a great deal and has taken an interest in ESP research of late. This is because all her life she has had experiences with the psychic and has accepted these incidents as part of her personality. Since she was a child she has had a recurring dream of a Chinese invasion. Before President John F. Kennedy was assassinated, she had visions of the event and tried to warn him, writing to Pierre Salinger, but to no avail.

Another vision that disturbs her greatly concerns the White House. At first she sees it as it is, and then she sees the whole front crumbling. Why this happens she does not understand, but to her this presents a frightening image.

Robert G. is a prosperous and well-liked dentist in the northeastern United States. Psychic experiences in his life are so numerous he no longer keeps track of all of them. About 80 percent of his premonitions actually come true; these range from very minor forecasts of events to happen in the near future, to major situations. Being a trained medical man, he naturally takes a scientific interest in this talent of his. He makes it a practice to clear his mind after going to bed and to wait for what might come through. Sometimes he gets nothing; at other times he gets many impressions rapidly. Many of his premonitions come completely unsought, but these are not so numerous as the items he has received while deliberately making himself available for such messages. He predicted that Jackie Kennedy would marry Aristotle Onassis at a time when that seemed most unlikely. Shortly after John Kennedy's assassination, just as Oswald had been captured, the doctor's wife asked what would happen next, and before he thought about what he was saying, he replied that Oswald would be shot at the police station. Not all his premonitions concern world events. In 1957, when he was still in the navy, stationed at St. Albans Naval Hospital, he and several fellow officers found themselves aboard the uss *Independence* as it was being completed at the Brooklyn Navy Yard. The men were walking around inspecting the ship, and suddenly Dr. G. heard an inner voice say, "You are going to get orders to get aboard that ship." His spirits sagged because he had always hated carriers, and he turned to the others and said, "Oh hell, I'm getting orders to go aboard that thing!" Everyone stopped and wondered how he knew, and Dr. G. had to invent an innocuous answer in order to get off the hook. Word got around among his fellow officers, and everyone started to kid him about this. About ten days later his orders did come and the captain of the *Independence* demanded to know who had tipped him off.

There were several other, more personal predictions of future events, all of which have come true. As far as the future is concerned, Dr. G. has some definite statements to make. He foresees the death of Elizabeth Taylor; he does not give any date for this, so perhaps the actress will live a long time. These were predictions made to me in writing on May 25, 1969: "I see the next Apollo shot putting a man on the moon, but the man remaining in the command module will come back alone." This did not happen, but a near fatal accident did occur during that next Apollo venture. "A black cloud over Russia and the Near East. Bad times are in store for Russia."

I am always leery of people who contact me with reams of material pertaining to future predictions and then follow this up with letter after letter until I am literally inundated with material. My suspicion regarding the validity of such material is perhaps prejudice. I have found that, on occasion, even the prolific letter writer has something valuable to contribute to the study of paranormal occurrences. Every case, of course, must be judged individually. When I first heard of Richard D. McClintic, I was somewhat dubious because of the large amount of material he forwarded to me. This material represented a record of his ESP experiences to date, most of it verified by witnesses and, in the cases when his predictions had come true, data pertaining to the objective reality of his predictions.

Mr. McClintic first got in touch with me on August 7, 1968. He is of relatively humble background. He had worked at various odd jobs, had been a factory worker and the owner of a coin-operated self-service laundry, and had spent two years in the army.

Mr. McClintic does not seek fame and has requested that I keep his address confidential. He lives in the Midwest. He is apparently not in need of funds and has for some time owned a small apartment house. His interest in extrasensory perception is one of curiosity, and he is not given to making professional use of his psychic ability. But he has played the stock market now and again, with excellent results; this he credits to his extrasensory perception since he doesn't have any personal knowledge of the stock market. As a young man, he lived in old houses and saw what he describes as ghosts. He has had ESP incidents all his life, ranging from foreknowledge of when a certain letter would arrive to his alleged ability to find money when he needed it—that is to say, he would relax and concentrate on money when he found that he needed some additional funds, and within a matter of days he would indeed either find money in the street or come into possession of unexpected funds. Much of his precognitive material comes in the dream state. He has had many experiences of astral projection—that, leaving his body and being conscious of having left it. On occasion, when he was very relaxed, he was able to "look through walls." He was able to experiment with this at will after a while; by looking straight ahead and visualizing a house that he could not normally see, he found himself suddenly viewing a scene in which a neighbor, an old lady living out of sight but close by, was just lighting her lamp. A moment later he jumped up and ran around the corner to a spot from where he could observe his neighbor. Sure enough, there she was, having just lit the lamp.

There is no doubt in my mind that Mr. McClintic is a medium. He does not wish to discuss his mediumship in his own surroundings for fear of being ridiculed or worse. His reasons for contacting me were mainly to have someone to talk to, and to get some sort of explanation for what had happened to him over the years. This, of course, I was happy to supply.

Mr. McClintic is somewhat doubtful about his predictions—he cannot put the time element on them, as he phrases it. He doesn't wish to be recognized as a prophet, but he feels impelled to communicate his views of the future to someone like myself. I should like to reemphasize that this is not a disturbed individual in any sense but simply a puzzled person who has the gift of second sight and doesn't know what to do about it. Here then are some of his predictions and my comments as to their verifications.

On August 7, 1968, Mr. McClintic foresaw that Jackie Kennedy would be married again. This, of course, happened some time after the date of the prediction. Also on August 7, 1968, Mr. McClintic stated, "I see a big train crash. I saw this as I was sitting staring at nothing. Cars seemed to be going down an embankment. Maybe in Ohio or some other state with an O in it, perhaps Oregon." On August 14, 1968, *The Republic,* a Columbus, Indiana, newspaper, reported, "Seventeen cars of a Penn-Central freight train, seven of them loaded with 150 mm howitzer shells and fuses, derailed in a residential area here today, forcing evacuation of about 3,500 persons. A railroad spokesman said the 100-car freight train was en route from Columbus, Ohio, to Richmond, Indiana." The wreck occurred near the town of Urbana, Ohio.

At the height of the McCarthy-for-President boom, when it was not at all decided whether Hubert Humphrey would become the Democratic candidate, Richard McClintic predicted that Humphrey would win at Chicago and that McCarthy would lose. Mr. McClintic added on August 8, 1968, "I don't think General Dwight D. Eisenhower will be alive a year from now." He wasn't.

Perhaps there is something more than personal ESP involved when Richard McClintic makes his predictions. Could it be he is aided by some discarnate personalities who see in him a channel of communication? I suspect that his mediumship, incomplete and undeveloped though it may be, is being used by those on the Other Side who wish to let us in the flesh know of what is in store. At any rate, here is what happened to Richard McClintic when he tried to meditate on the outcome of the presidential election. This was in August of 1968, and here are his own words as to how he felt:

Before the Indiana primary, I had tried to find out who would be the next president of the United States. I went to New York in my mind and tried to feel or hear who would be president, if indeed he came from New York. I seemed to be trying to go through a curtain or time barrier. At first I could not get Robert Kennedy or any of the other men who might want to be president. Finally, after holding on to Robert Kennedy's name and Mayor John Lindsay's name, I got another name. It was Lederman or Ladman. I thought he was a senator a few years back, this being when I was trying to find out the next president's name. I felt some things about Robert Kennedy and also John Lindsay and Richard Nixon, but I couldn't put them into words. It was as if the words were just beyond me, and also the name of the president, and as if it was there waiting for me but wasn't really ready or decided yet for sure. Maybe it was, and the picture had not yet moved into my mind, but was rather outside or just beyond it. I think the next president will be from New York City, as earlier, but I still don't know what Ladman or Lederman means. About five weeks ago I had a dream in which a girl who works at a local library and I were talking. I told her that Roosevelt was a great man and that I just loved him. I then said that the liberals got in, and then the conservatives; and that was the end of the dream. Yesterday I lay down and found myself saying, 'Roosevelt, Roosevelt,' about three or four times before I caught myself. I might have been in a light trance state.

The senator to whom Mr. McClintic refers was Senator Herbert Lehman, and Franklin D. Roosevelt is not inconceivable as a communicator, for he knew very well the reality of psychic communication. President Roosevelt had communications with his deceased mother, Sara Delano, and was at all times fascinated by psychic research. Far-fetched though this may seem to some, could it not be that the late Senator Lehman and the late President Roosevelt were trying to communicate something about the future to Richard McClintic? Both men were liberal Democrats and might have considered Mr. McClintic a likely channel.

Apparently the first contact with me proved fruitful in that it stimulated other psychic material in Richard McClintic. At any rate, he communicated with me again, on August 10, 1968: "There will be more riots in Cleveland, Ohio, and Mayor Stokes will have difficulty. For president on the Democratic ticket, I see Hubert Humphrey. The Democrats will be having troubles at the convention—revolt, it seems, and a walkout. The Republicans will win; maybe Richard Nixon. George Wallace will hurt the Democrats more than the Republicans. Indiana Democratic Senator Birch Bayh will be reelected." Of course, every one of these predictions came true. Mr. McClintic can hardly be called a political analyst, and it seems to me amazing that he should pinpoint with such accuracy what was to transpire somewhat later.

After I encouraged Mr. McClintic to keep exact records of his visions and dreams, he contacted me again from time to time. On August 15, 1968, I had this statement from him: "The Supreme Court won't have any new members until after elections. Chief Court Justice Warren will stay as temporary chief justice." This, of course, came to pass. "More riots next year, also scattered fights with some gangs involved and shooting between small groups of blacks and whites. It doesn't seem to be too serious. Some of the riots will be against the city or police, and they will be more serious." The UPI reported from

Louisville, Kentucky, under dateline of August 15, 1968—that is twelve hours after Mr. McClintic had filed his prediction— "Groups of Negro youths looted and tossed rocks and bottles and three police cruisers were fired on from passing cars Wednesday night, as violence broke out in a square-mile area of the city's west end." In this case perhaps Mr. McClintic merely picked up events already transpiring at a distance. "More student protests at colleges this coming school year. This includes the school year starting 1969 in January. Watch for strikes by teachers in high schools. Students are going to picket and stay away from schools in support of them in some cities and areas. This may be very scattered, but later on it could be catching on. In future years, some students may strike schools the way unions strike companies." This did indeed occur.

Also on August 15, 1968, Mr. McClintic wrote, "Ronald Reagan can be governor of California again if he wants it. He can have a place in the Republican national administration, if he wants it. I don't think he will. He has presidential ambitions."

On September 20, 1968, well ahead of the national elections, Mr. McClintic predicted Richard Nixon the winner. He also foretold that George Wallace would hurt Humphrey's chances in the North. Also on September 20, 1968, Mr. McClintic predicted that J. Edgar Hoover was near the end of his career as director of the FBI, and that Director of Selective Service General Hershey was on the way out, but not before 1969, and perhaps even then that he would have another year or two. Both of these predictions came to pass.

On September 24, 1968, Richard McClintic predicted, "Dissent is here to stay. There won't be a police state over the next few years, but laws will be tightened somewhat. No war between whites and Negroes, but Negro extremists are plotting to cause trouble. The blowing up of bridges and buildings, statues, and other places—like important landmarks and buildings—is one thing they have been discussing. Also how to start a civil war. They are also thinking of shooting a few moderate Negroes, to warn Negroes to stay away from whites and liberals. But most Negroes want to join the American society, not blow it up, so most of these moves will fail." That dissent is here to stay we know all too well. "American space race will start to slow down again. Troubles in the rocket are part of the trouble." This was said a year and a half before the Apollo mission ran into trouble with an engine malfunction and was forced to return to earth for one of the moon missions. "Alexander Dubcek to leave Communist Party leadership within the next two years. The Russians want him to go, but will wait and bide their time until they have more of what they want." This also came to pass. Step by step Dubcek was first removed from his premiership, then from his other posts, and finally from the Communist leadership altogether. "Egypt's Nasser will call another Arab council within the next few months. He wants more money among other things from the oil-producing countries of Arabs, so he can have more money to use against Israel." This transpired about a year after the prediction was made.

On November 11, 1968, Richard McClintic predicted, "Another earthquake in Iran and Turkey. Buildings will be destroyed. This will happen any time after December first of 1968." It happened early in 1970, and it was a disastrous earthquake. As always, pinpointing the time element seems nearly impossible for psychics. This is due to the fact that time as we know it is nonexistent in the fourth dimension. Also on November 11, 1968, Mr. McClintic predicted, "More fighting in Vietnam. The Reds aren't going to give up easily. Nixon will try to end the war, but the Reds won't quit except on their own terms. They will come through Laos; also they will bother other South Asian countries more. Americans soldiers will be in South Asia for a while yet. There will be more troubles with Reds on the frontiers of Thailand." The invasion of Cambodia and fighting in Laos are now a matter of record. Most of these events transpired only in 1970. There was no way of guessing at them as early as December of 1968, when this prediction was made.

Also in September of 1968, Mr. McClintic predicted, "There will be bomb scares in stores in some large cities, including New York City." This has happened since. These were more than scares; several bombs exploded in leading department stores in New York.

Of course, Mr. McClintic has been wrong some of the time. For instance, he persistently predicted the first landing on the moon in 1973. However, on August 15, 1968, Mr. McClintic predicted some sort of atomic accident in Soviet Russia. "Nasser is going to have troubles with students, also plots by army men against him." This came to pass when a plot of officers not in sympathy with his policies was discovered and squashed. Prophetically, Richard McClintic wrote on January 18, 1969: "Senator Fulbright will hit at Republicans and also members of his own party about the war in South Vietnam and also the money to be spent to rearm America." Years later Senator Fulbright did head a movement to cut funds from the government for spending in Vietnam. "Barbra Streisand to win a movie Oscar." She certainly did, in 1970.

"Riots in Japan this year between radical students and the government. The Japanese premier should be careful; his safety is in danger." This also is a matter of record.

With so much material pertaining to what was then the future having already been realized, I turn to Mr. McClintic's predictions pertaining to the future that have not yet come to pass. In reporting these visions, I do not assume responsibility for their accuracy, of course; but it stands to reason that some of them may indeed come true as made, since many, although not all, of his earlier predictions have become reality. I hasten to add that I am convinced of Mr. McClintic's sincerity, that he does not use sources other than himself in making these statements, and that he has nothing to gain from making them. Other than that, I find him merely one of many amateur prophets living quietly in this country, working at their chosen profession or job, and watching with some fascination their talent for what it may be worth—to themselves, perhaps very little; to those of us who report such apparently unusual occurrences, they are markers on the road to the recognition of what man is all about.

On August 7, 1968, McClinic predicted that there would be a breakthrough with an atomic engine—a flying engine powered by atomic energy. He also predicted a new cure, or improvement, for some kind of blood disease. Mr. McClintic also predicted an attempted murder of the shah of Iran. In a vision he actually saw the shah getting out of his car and someone trying to kill him. This has not yet come to pass. On August 10, 1968, Mr. McClintic forecast an attempted revolt in Cuba. It didn't seem to be serious and looked to him more like a planned revolt than an actual one. At the same time he foresaw Castro leaving the scene as leader of Cuba.

About the Near Eastern conflict Mr. McClintic got this information from his psychic sources in the late 1960s: "Israel is eyeing atomic weapons. She could make them, and in time she probably will. She thinks Russia will promise the Arabs that she will help them out next time around, and she doesn't believe the United States will help Israel. Still, Russia won't give atomic bombs to the Arabs; she doesn't trust them." Mr. McClintic also predicted the loss of an American atomic-powered submarine. He saw this happening somewhere in very deep waters. "The captain is in his late twenties or early thirties, has dark hair, and is married; and there are at least 110 or more men aboard, and it won't be recovered." The number in his vision was U145, or something similar.

Mr. McClintic predicted that Spain would have a king again, but England would not give up Gibraltar. In September of 1968 Mr. McClintic predicted, "Russia will not be our enemy forever. They are afraid of a united Germany, but have more to fear from a strong China with atomic bombs and missiles and the H-bomb. There will not be a Russian and Chinese war during the next three years. Perhaps small border fights." These small border skirmishes did take place, and ostensibly Russia and China are again at peace, although what lies ahead no one can guess.

On September 24, 1968, Mr. McClintic indicated that there was a Russian spy ring operating in the United States and that two of the agents were posing as Americans, using the names of dead Americans or of people living in other cities. The FBI would be on their trail, and one ring would break within the next year. One team was a man and wife. On the other hand, Mr. McClintic also spoke of a Russian in Russia working for the CIA, who, however, will be caught by the Russians. His name had the letters *I* and *B* in it, and he would be given a closed trial when caught, without Western reporters present.

In another list of predictions, obtained during meditation on October 10, 1968, Mr. McClintic spoke of "the Arabs [being] interested in buying material to make atomic bombs. A story will break about this in the future, next year." In another part of the world Mr. McClintic foresaw nothing but troubles. "Tunisia and Saudi Arabia will complain about CIA activities in their countries, and African countries with black governments will step up warfare against the Portuguese colonies." He elaborated on this on November 11, 1968: "More trouble in Africa. The blacks will attack the white countries by small groups of soldiers into the south. No peace here but more small actions of fighting. More fighting in Nigeria. Both sides are getting outside armies to help them. Also fighting in Rhodesia. This is a small band of soldiers entering from other countries. Also more fighting in the countries Portugal owns in Africa."

Even England would not be free of violence and dissent, he predicted. "A bomb blows up in Merrie Old England. Nationalists are mixed up in this. They will be caught, and more than one bomb goes off." On January 16, 1969, Mr. McClintic predicted, "More planes and other equipment will be sold to Israel besides the fifty planes promised them. The United States will sell her planes and another country will sell her parts, equipment, and other material. West Germany will help her in some way, either by bank loans or in other financial ways." Again Mr. McClintic received some impressions about the future of Great Britain: "The royal family of England should be careful; enemies may try to harm them. When elections come to England, Labour will be kicked out of office. Prime Minister Wilson and his party have stepped on too many people, and people want and will get a change."

Under dateline of January 18, 1969, Mr. McClintic predicted that Governor Wallace would again try for the presidency in 1972, as would President Nixon. He said that "Eastern Europe will become more liberal despite the Russians. Russia won't go back to the Joseph Stalin days of big trials and untold numbers of people shipped to prison camps and sentenced to death." To this he added, on January 28, 1969: "A shakeup in the Russian leadership in the next fifteen months. At least one is to be demoted, maybe more. New men will be given more important jobs. Some bureaus of the government will be shaken up. The Russians will claim to have caught more American spies in the next few months. Also someone with the initial *S* will be given more power in the Communist Party leadership of Russia." Auguring even more destruction in the wars and skirmishes of the future, Mr. McClintic predicts the invention of a laser gun that kills and can destroy entire tanks. Also he sees a weapon that can make sections of the air or space blow up without shelling, on the principle of the atomic bomb but working across distances.

To balance this dire news, he foresees a machine that heals or makes well sections of the human body. This machine will do the job of nature when it is perfected. It will speed up nature's processes of healing. What I found particularly interesting was Mr. McClintic's statement that a way would be found "to grow people in gardens, or at least start them in so-called gardens like nurseries." He also speaks of means to keep people from aging and of new methods of leaving Earth. He speaks of antigravity devices, machines that can reverse gravity; and he also foresees a device that can read people's thoughts. Most of the latter predictions sounded more in the "Star Trek" category than that which we may reasonably expect in the near future, but I pass them on for the record. One must never forget that a television set or a radio would have seemed mighty improbable to someone of, let us say, the sixteenth or seventeenth century.

Mr. McClintic's volume of predictions and his vast amount of psychic experiences over the years would qualify him for inclusion in my list of prophets, major or minor; but he is not a professional in any sense of the word. He is pleased with his amateur status, and in his last communication to me he decided to "lay off prophesying for a while." Amateur prophets have less of a motive to look into the future and to make statements about it. They have more to lose by admitting extraordinary powers of perception. They are being ridiculed in many cases, their sanity is attacked, and their personal lives are threatened by the very fact that they are different from most others around them. Professional psychics do not have this problem. They are reconciled to the idea of being different. They make a business, or at least a calling, out of their talents, and accept the good along with the bad. But the amateur prophet has a soft shell. He has no defense. That is why so few amateur prophets have come forward to tell their stories. When they come to me, they find a sympathetic ear. I publish their accounts, if they are verifiable and honest and if they so desire. I protect them from the curious and from members of the media who like to prey on them and publish sensational stories. The press, by and large, is not too friendly to serious psychic research. It prefers to tell the story in terms of exploitable personalities.

I would like to encourage anyone with the qualifications of an amateur prophet to practice this talent and to come forward and record his prophetic experiences with either me or others interested in the subject.

A California housewife by the name of Margaret McKinley has had psychic experiences most of her adult life. She came
to see me in Hollywood on April 15, 1970, because of the disturbing impact some of her visions had made upon her. She
felt she should communicate these impressions to me for whatever use I might wish to make of them. There were also elements of reincarnation in her narrative, and I decided to see
her in person and, if necessary, to put her into a hypnotic
trance state, possibly to regress her to any previous lives, if such
could be proved. It turned out to be something along those
lines, except that her incarnations seem to be in the future.
But I had better report my meeting with Margaret McKinley
as it progressed step by step.

*Mrs. McKinley, what are the recent events that made you feel that
you ought to talk to me?*
"Well, there's several things. One is, I keep seeing a symbol.
And it's kind of a *Y* turned upside down, and then it has two
circles with dots in the middle, and then a small *a* and a large
M. Now, I've been seeing it for quite some time. Then I get
the feeling that I'm standing *above* the world and I can look
down on the world and see everything that's going on."
Is this while awake or while asleep?
"Both."
Is this astral projection?
"No, because I know everything that's going on. I'm sitting
there and I can still see myself reading a book; I can feel my
feet on the floor."
*Do you get any information in this condition that you would not
normally have?*
"Yes, I do. One was about the astronauts."
What about them?
"Monday morning, about three o'clock in the morning, I was
sitting on the couch, and I just felt myself growing, and all of
a sudden I could see the astronauts, and they were having *trou-*

ble; they were calling for help. But then, all of a sudden it disappeared and I didn't think anything about it because everything with the flight was going so smoothly. And then, Monday *night,* I heard on TV that they were having trouble."

Was this the only time you had this kind of impression?

"I was at work, in '68, when I could hear my father calling me, and then *all of a sudden* I felt myself 'growing,' and I saw him lying in the hospital; he had had a heart attack and was almost dead."

Did he notice you at the time when you had this feeling?

"Yes, he did."

How did he notice you?

"He said he saw me standing there, and that he knew that I wasn't there yet, but that I would be."

You told me the first time we met that you had some inkling of a neighborhood murder prior to its happening.

"My mother was here from Indiana and my husband was working nights, and my daughter and my mother and I were already in bed. It was dark, and I closed my eyes and then all of a sudden I saw this man standing over me with a knife. I opened my eyes real fast, but I didn't see anything so I started to go back to sleep, and then I saw him again. This time I got up, and I thought maybe somebody had gotten in the house, but we searched and didn't find anyone. I thought, If I leave a light on, I probably won't see it, but I *did.* This was about ten o'clock at night. The next morning my daughter heard on the TV that a woman had been stabbed *at the time that I saw this.*"

Did the man who did the stabbing correspond to the vision you had had of him?

"Yes, he did."

You saw his picture afterwards?

"Yes."

What about the time?

"It was the exact time, ten o'clock at night."

How far away from your house?

"About fifteen miles."
In recent times have you had any unsought previsions of world events of any kind?
"About a year ago I was lying in bed with a fever and fell asleep. I saw myself traveling different planets. When I got to this one, there were seven people standing on top of a mountain. They were looking out across the valley to another mountain and talking in a language I didn't know. Then they noticed me and turned around. Now, this place, they said it was *Earth*, and it was as if a blast had burned everything out."
How did you know it was Earth if you didn't understand their language?
"I felt it was Earth. It was just that feeling that it was Earth and that this is going to happen, and it wouldn't be too distant from now."
You said you had a fever. What sort of illness was it?
"I had the Hong-Kong flu."
Would you say that this vision was connected with your illness?
"I asked the doctor about it and he said my fever wasn't that bad."
What happened after this particular vision?
"I woke up. I could still see the buildings—what was left of them—smouldering."
What part of the Earth was it?
"Well, it looked like the United States, like California."
And did you get any impression of when this happened?
"It seemed like it was about 1980. It is just a feeling because I felt quite a few years older."
Did you see any particular clothes on yourself or on the seven people?
"Yes, they were long, below the knees, the skirts; they were in rags, because they said that they had been in the blast, but had survived it."
Anything else about this you remember?
"When they turned around and spoke, it seemed that I could understand them. I was talking one language and they were

talking another, and they said that there had been an *atomic blast*; I could just understand those few words."
What did it sound like?
"It sounded kind of like Egyptian."
It didn't sound like any current language?
"No."
Did the people look like ordinary people whom you know?
"No. They were a lot taller and a lot slimmer, and their eyes were funny, the pupils of their eyes were of a yellow color, and the whites of their eyes were pink."
Did you have other visions pertaining to world events?
"Three weeks ago I was lying in bed and closed my eyes, and I saw myself, all at the same time, but I was in four different incarnations. I was in Ancient Egypt, then I was in the Old West, and I was in the present, and then I was in the future."
Did you look the same?
"No, I was dressed for each period."
Have you ever had memories of having lived before?
"About two weeks ago I was sitting in my living room reading a book about astrology. All of a sudden I could see myself in Egypt, and I saw a man all dressed in black robes. I had seen him several times in visions, and he kept saying, 'You've got to come back, you've got to come back.' The day I saw myself there he said, 'Well, you finally got back. Now you can take your place and stay here again.' It seemed he was speaking in English."
Have you ever had any feeling of having been to a place before that you haven't been?
"When I lived in Canada, I went to a house, and it seemed as if I had lived there before. I knew where everything was."
Did you recognize anyone you might have known in another life?
"Yes, the owner of the house in Canada. We talked with one another as if we had known one another forever. She called me by name, and it wasn't my name; it was *Amdra*."
Any reason?

"She said she knew me by that name, and she said that I had lived in that house about 200 years ago."
What made her think that?
"She said she had just seen me there. At the time I didn't believe in reincarnation, but after I started getting these flashes, I started asking questions."
Since then have you had similar flashes?
"Yes; I could see carriages, and people walking around, and they seemed rather plain."
Could you see yourself?
"Yes, I could."
Did you look different from what you look today?
"No, except for the clothes."
You had the same face?
"Yes."
"Have you ever gotten information in this way about the name that you had at that time, or the dates or the town?
"There was a man who said that it was 1754. His name was Henry."
You mean this is a man you met in Canada?
"He was a butler."
Have you had any other flashes of earlier lives?
"Yes, it seems I lived on another planet. I'll be sitting outdoors at night and watching Mars, and all of a sudden a thought will come into my mind, Why am I not *back home* on Mars instead of here? My husband has said several times I have talked in my sleep in a language he has never heard."
Any other lives?
"When I was little, I always talked about living in Egypt a long time ago. I would say that I should be living here in the year 2000. And that I just wasn't wearing the right kind of clothes that kids wore then."
In the future?
"Yes."
[At this point I put Mrs. McKinley into hypnotic trance.]

What year is this?
"Seventeen hundred."
What town are you in?
"Cairo."
What is your name?
"Maidra."
Is there anyone else there?
"A man. High priest."
What is he doing?
"Teaching me."
What is he teaching you?
"High priestess."
Where is the teaching taking place?
"Temple of Râ."
Can you see yourself in another existence?
"No."
All right, then come forward now, into the present. Go into the future, until you see yourself in a lifetime after this. What is your name?
"Maatha." [sic]
Where do you live?
"The planet Venus."
What year is this?
"Two thousand one hundred."
What happened to Earth?
"It was destroyed."
What year?
"Nineteen ninety-five."
How was it destroyed?
"A nuclear bomb."
Who did it?
"Everybody!"
Why?
"Foolish hate."
What country started it?
"France."

What happened to America?
"Bombed."
Is nothing left?
"No."
Are there any people left?
"Very few."
Where do they live?
"In a cave at the top of the mountain."
Where?
"Colorado."
And how do the people get to Venus?
"Space ships."
Where are the space ships from?
"Mars, Venus."
Did they come to take the people off the earth?
"Yes."
Can you speak their language?
"No; they speak our language."
How many years is their lifetime?
"Nine hundred years."
All right, I want you to go back again to the present, into your present lifetime, and to rest.

Even if we are to take a skeptical view of the material relating to Venus and Mars, who is to say that Mrs. McKinley's frightening picture of atomic destruction was not a true vision of things to come? Or a warning of what *might* be?

Chapter 3

International Prophecy of World Events

When a major event affecting the entire globe is in the making, could it not be that people with prophetic vision become aware of it in various parts of our world?

While it is also true that prophecy tends to focus primarily on events, areas, and people of greater interest to the prophets where they live, in the case of catastrophes of major impact there do not seem to be such geographical limitations.

It is not clear to me why people receive these advance "screenings" of events to come when they are not in a position to do anything to prevent them.

But perhaps the challenge lies in telling others about their prophecies, others who *can* affect the outcome . . . if they so desire.

In this chapter I will report some remarkable prophetic visions and prophecies, all well documented and researched.

When a medium or psychic person predicts events or conditions that can be observed or corroborated by more than one person, especially the public at large, we are dealing with phenomena essentially different from the personal prediction of the psychic reader or, at the lowest level, the fortune-teller. For it is one thing for such a person to foretell an event in the private life of a person coming for a consultation, an event that has meaning for and can be properly experienced only by that person, and another to predict a world "happening" that may concern many people in many ways.

For example, let us examine the strange thing that happened to two German reporters, J. B. Hutton and Joachim Brandt. As Hutton reported in a book dealing with his experiences, the two newsmen were sent in the spring of 1932 to do a picture story about the Hamburg-Altona shipyards which were then in full activity. They were shown around the yards by one of the executives, and the afternoon passed quickly. As they were about to leave, both men distinctly heard the thunder of many airplanes overhead, and soon the *ack-ack* of anti-aircraft guns blotted out the noises of the shipyard. It was dark by now, and the two reporters observed the explosions of many bombs.

At first, they thought they were seeing a practice alarm. But as flames engulfed the area, the two frightened reporters realized that the battle was raging in earnest. Fire trucks raced past them.

Suddenly, all was quiet. They decided to go back and offer their help. All the while Brandt had been taking pictures.

At the gates they were brusquely told not to bother. In fact, they were threatened by the guards, so they decided to drive back into Hamburg.

The sky had been dark during the aerial attack, but now, as they regained the quietness of Hamburg's streets, they noticed that all was normally lit and the people were going about their business in an ordinary manner. They halted the car, got out, and looked back toward the shipyards. The darkness had lifted and the yards were intact!

Their editor accused them of drunkenness, especially when Brandt's photographs showed nothing unusual. The two men decided it was the better part of valor to keep quiet about their experience, except with immediate family and friends.

Hutton went to England just before World War II erupted. There, in 1943, he saw a newspaper report of a highly successful aerial attack by the Royal Air Force on Hamburg's shipyards. On investigation he realized that the scene he and Brandt had witnessed in 1932 had become reality eleven years later *in every detail!*

In a way, precognitive experiences differ little from retrocognition, that is, the reliving of events after they have happened, in full detail, by persons who are not familiar with them or in any way subject to suggestions about them. The mechanics of seeing into the future are definitely related to the ability to peer into the past. The psychic "apparatus" within man is brought into play in both phenomena, but we can accept hindsight more readily than foresight—that which *was* has, after all, already happened, but that which is yet to be has not occurred, and how can one experience something that is not yet in existence?

In both precognitions and retrocognition, and also in cases of simultaneous experience of an event happening at a distance, we are dealing with displacements in time and/or space that require a totally new approach to our understanding of the nature of time.

Perhaps the most famous of the retrocognitive experiences is the case of two Englishwomen named Moberly and Jourdain who visited the gardens of Versailles some years ago and suddenly found themselves present at a garden party for Marie Antoinette, an event that actually transpired in the eighteenth century. They have written a book about their experience entitled *An Adventure*. There also are many comments in print—by people to whom it didn't happen—trying to explain the phenomenon.

Less well known is the case of a woman on a holiday in Dunkirk some years after World War II who witnessed the aerial attack on the port city during the retreat of the Allied Forces. Again, the experience was so real to the subject that she thought the town was being attacked in a renewal of warfare.

These experiences are not hallucinations in the medical sense; that is, they are not fabrications of a disturbed mind. They are like tuning in on a radio or television broadcast from the past—except that the receiver is in your head!

While in China, early in 1939, an American war correspondent named F. S. Cook had a dream that he was at Waikiki Beach and the air was filled with Japanese planes; he saw himself running toward the harbor—Pearl Harbor—only to see it filled with burning warships.

Some precognitive experiences occur during waking hours, but many more arise in the dream state, when conscious thought is temporarily suspended and the intuitive—psychic—forces bear upon the unconscious part of man's personality.

Abraham Lincoln saw himself in a coffin in the very room of the White House where his coffin later stood, and he described his precognitive experience to a number of people.

Jess Stearn, my good friend and a fellow author, has delved into this subject without previous convictions one way or another and has written about many such cases in his books, notably *Door to the Future*.

Years ago in a magazine article, he reported his interview with psychic Helen Stalls. Three days before Kennedy's death she "saw" him being assassinated.

But what about the amateur psychic, the reluctant medium who has strong impressions of future events and communicates them only with misgivings, not wishing to derive any gain whatever? What about these predictions that seem to arise from a genuine psychic experience?

The following case history deals with a child—a rare case, but deliberately chosen because it is particularly puzzling, for a child is not capable of sophisticated tactics of deceit nor possessed of knowledge of the world around him to the degree of an adult. Thus anything of the supernormal coming through such a channel would seem purer and more worthy of study than premonitions coming through the more developed personality of an adult.

John Scherer and his wife were the parents of a boy, also called John. Mr. Scherer was a tool-and-die-maker, had two years of college, and served in the U.S. Navy from 1946 to 1949. He had premonitory experiences on several occasions, such as dreams accurately picturing ports he had never been to, foreknowledge of an automobile accident, and a strong awareness of danger. All of these ESP experiences were verified.

Mrs. Scherer had no psychic abilities to speak of, but her older sister had strong premonitory feelings prior to illness, trouble, or other emotional events in her family.

Thus, a certain amount of inherited ESP potential was certainly present in their child, John, who at age two startled his parents by predicting the sex and birth date of their second child. At the age of five, the boy spoke of an earthquake due in Japan, complaining that he already "felt" it. The earthquake occurred a month later.

After the parents became aware of their son's unusual talent, they encouraged it and would question him from time to time about future events. But they never prodded him in any way. There were a number of lesser incidents involving ESP, not all of them involving the future but sometimes dealing with events at a distance otherwise unknowable at the time. The boy's ability to foresee events was stronger in the first half of the month, i.e., during the period of the waxing moon.

The Scherers paid me a visit on May 19, 1965, and I found little John no more brilliant than any other six-year-old boy.

He wasn't particularly cooperative, perhaps because I was a stranger to him.

One of the predictions the boy had made at that time concerned an earthquake in California. He "saw" a blimp hovering nearby which later exploded. When I asked for further details, the boy elaborated. A tall building with a big clock, mountains in the background, small buildings around the clock tower, and a small island opposite the clock. He then drew a picture of the scene.

Immediately Mr. Scherer recognized it as the ferry building at the end of Market Street in San Francisco—an area the boy had never seen. The child also predicted that a volcano would erupt in the mountains slightly northwest of a spot he indicated on a map—the Pikes Peak area.

"He has trouble with dates," his mother explains. Small wonder if even older mediums have this problem.

On July 30, 1965, the boy announced that he saw a Hawaiian volcano erupt at an hour when it would be daylight in Hawaii but night on the west coast. It did not happen, however. Was he seeing it out of our time context? Only the future can tell if these predictions, so far unrealized, are figments of imagination or genuine previsions incorrectly interpreted as to their place in our time stream.

Are some events, especially tragedies, so strong that they cast an emotional shadow ahead of themselves, a shadow more than one psychic person can notice?

On October 21, 1966, an avalanche of coal waste rolled down into the little Welsh town of Aberfan, engulfing in its course a school filled with children who had just said their customary prayers. Almost two hundred people were killed in the disaster, most of them school children, and the town of Aberfan became quiet with desolation. But was the disaster really unforeseen in the psychic sense?

The story of the tragedy went around the world many times, arousing great sympathy everywhere and giving birth to relief funds and other charitable enterprises. The London weekly *Psychic News* reacted in a different way to the event, gathering up the many predictions made concerning the catastrophe.

Most prominent among those who *knew* something of this sort was imminent was my good friend Michael Bentine, a television personality. Michael, who has had many psychic experiences, was taping a segment of his television series, "All Square," on the day before the Welsh disaster. One of the comedy sketches in it concerned a Welsh mining town and referred to its black hills and, in a funny spoof on *How the West Was Won*, had American Indians attack the Welsh miners.

But on the afternoon of the taping, Michael felt physically ill at the prospect of doing the sketch. He insisted that it be replaced with another skit on a different topic and with a different locale. But this was impossible at such short notice, and Bentine reluctantly went through with the sketch. Fortunately, the show was not to be telecast until the following week, so the producers were able to eliminate the sketch after the Aberfan disaster happened the next day.

Michael Bentine was not the only one who sensed disaster. One day ahead of the event, a woman working with the Oxford Psychophysical Research Unit had a terrifying dream in which she saw people being engulfed by dirt and coal slag. Two women in Kent had dreams involving children being buried in underground tunnels, and Mr. M. Hennessey, of Barnstaple, Devon, saw children trying to climb out of a room, followed by the sight of people running to where the children had been.

A Lancaster man named J. Arthur Taylor dreamed he was in the town of Pontypridd, buying a book, when suddenly he saw the word *Aberfan* in large letters before his eyes, and as he looked closer he saw desolate houses and streets. All this happened before the event, and was vouched for by local newspapers publishing these accounts. Moreover, a little school child drew a picture of the disaster in class the day *before* it happened—complete in every detail, including a school clock showing the exact moment of sad truth!

All the people mentioned here made their anxieties known to someone near them, even though the mass media became interested only *after* the fact. But so it must be so long as extrasensory perception remains a stepchild of science.

Jimmy Jacobs was the son of a Dutch meat wholesaler. He has had the gift of prediction since the age of five. He served in the Royal Air Force during World War II and later went into show business. Eventually he became the prosperous owner of the Gargoyle Club in Soho, one of the best-known London cabarets. Every year a list of his predictions for the following year was announced to the press and the old predictions list checked for accuracy.

On December 31, 1965, the *East London Advertiser* published a statement by Jacobs to the effect that in 1966 an avalanche in South America would kill seventeen people. In a dispatch from Rio de Janeiro dated January 11, 1966, published by the *London Evening Standard,* concerning a flood disaster in Brazil, the following paragraph stands out:

> Police said that seventeen people, including many children, were feared dead after many houses in the Copacabana Beach suburb collapsed under the weight of water cascading down from the mountains which pin Rio against the sea.

On December 31, 1965, Jimmy Jacobs stated that a top impresario would die in the following year. Billy Rose died not long afterward.

Jacobs foresaw that another royal child would be born in 1966. Thirty days later, an announcement was made that Princess Alexandra was expecting her second child.

Long before the assassination of President Kennedy, Jacobs had felt that the president was in danger. He was so sure of this that he contacted the American Embassy in London but was told to forget it.

Mrs. Aldyn F. is a housewife living in San Luis Obispo, a coastal town in California halfway between San Francisco and Santa Barbara. She has had premonitions on occasion, mostly in the dream state. Not long ago, she dreamed that she was in a nearby town when a storm struck and the sea was rising higher and higher. She saw herself grab some children, telling them to get out of there quickly. Then the tidal wave struck and she saw the water rush through the streets.

When she woke up the next morning, she confided the vivid dream to her daughter. Her husband was out of the house at the time, but he soon returned with the paper. The headlines were all about a tidal wave that had struck a nearby town a few hours before.

Although Mrs. F. was able to state the facts only after the event had occurred, she had nevertheless experienced it simultaneously or perhaps even ahead of time.

Predictions can come from strange quarters. Some of the channels are professional mediums, others are housewives, still others may be amateur students of the occult. But one generally does not associate the education field with psychic phenomena, and yet I have met a number of teachers who have confided their unusual experiences to me. "Confided" is the right word, for there are prejudices beyond belief.

A Philadelphia schoolteacher living in what was obviously a haunted house had laboriously investigated the house's history, had consulted several mediums, and in general had attempted to explain scientifically the phenomena, for which there were several witnesses.

After describing the activities in her house on television, she was told by the board of education that parapsychology was not a fit subject to be discussed in their jurisdiction. They threatened her with the loss of her job if she opened her mouth again in public on the subject. Rather than submit to such medieval suppression of what she knew was true, the woman quit her teaching job.

Thus it was with some hesitancy that another teacher, Marianne Elko, approached me, for she had been subjected to ridicule and disbelief in her own surroundings whenever she spoke of her uncanny experiences. Mrs. Elko is a natural medium, one especially given to predictions and communications with the dead.

Mrs. Elko first contacted me, writing in her native German out of fear of having her mail read by someone who might cause her embarrassment, while I was appearing on one of my shows on Pittsburgh's station KDKA.

"For the past two years, since 1963," she wrote, "people have come to me from the spirit world, people I don't know personally. It is all very confusing to me. Some three years before the death of President Kennedy, I 'saw' his assassination. I can foresee events by as much as five to ten years."

It sounded interesting, even though I am cautious about people who claim, *after* the event, to have foretold the murder of Kennedy. But Mrs. Elko was no swindler, no publicity-mad person wanting to cash in on a special talent. She was shy and hesitant when I met her in Pittsburgh in October 1965.

The first thing I always ask people is when they first noticed anything unusual about themselves, so I asked the teacher when she had her first psychic experience, and with whom.

During World War II Mrs. Elko lived in Munich and Würzburg, Germany. Whenever she passed a certain building, she could see it as it would be *after* the bombs had hit. She avoided the building, of course, and within a matter of days, the building was hit and looked exactly as she had seen it in her visions.

She correctly predicted her brother's return from the war, although the family had been notified that he was missing in action.

"He will be home ten days hence," she said to her family, and on the tenth day the brother walked in.

In 1958, she predicted that John F. Kennedy would become president and she bet a friend, Dr. Rice of Pittsburgh, a nickel that Lyndon Johnson would be the vice president. The wager was promptly paid when the event transpired, two years later.

In 1962 she felt so strongly about the impending murder of the president that she tried to warn him, but a schoolteacher in a small Pennsylvania town was even less likely to succeed in this than Jeane Dixon, who knew a lot of important people in Washington and still failed to get through.

Mrs. Elko had a friend by the name of Kay Lehrmann, who worked for the public utility commission in Harrisburg. Through her Mrs. Elko tried to get an interview with the governor of Pennsylvania, but only managed to see an assistant. This was in July 1962, but nothing was done about her warning.

But, she claims, the late president was so grateful for her attempt to save him that he "came" to her on November 25, 1963, with the request that she transmit a message to his brothers. Among the evidence given her was a detailed description of a mirror in the house of the president's father at Hyannisport, Massachusetts, which consists of twenty-two compartments—evidently a hint that this numeral has mystic significance. On October 3, 1964, Mrs. Elko claims Kennedy requested that a certain inscription be placed on his grave, an inscription he described as existing already on a tombstone dated 1841 in Truro, on Cape Cod:

> *Then shall the dust return to the earth as it was; and the spirit shall return unto God who gave it.*

I have no idea whether this tombstone exists or not. If it does it would not in itself prove the identity of Mrs. Elko's communicator, of course.

President Kennedy was not the only world figure seeking her out. On April 1, 1963, she was sitting in her home when she suddenly heard a voice speak to her.

"Write it down," the voice commanded in German. With a trembling hand, Mrs. Elko obeyed. To her surprise, her handwriting changed to a style she had never seen before. Her visitor identified himself as the late and unlucky Emperor Charles of Austria, who had died in exile after World War I, forty years earlier.

In a soft Austrian accent, the caller informed her of many things, particularly of a war of total destruction that would befall mankind in 1988 if it was not averted by the concerted effort of all people of goodwill. The Berlin Wall, he said, would stay another eight years; and he asked her to write to a Dr. Arthur Werner in Vienna.

Mrs. Elko had never heard of this man, but she obeyed the spirit's order and, to her surprise, her letter was answered. There was such a man. All she had been given was the man's name and "Vienna VI." No street or number. I have seen the reply to this letter, in which Dr. Werner expressed *his* surprise at having heard from a stranger in Pennsylvania, but he admitted that he had been a close friend of the late emperor.

Dr. Werner welcomed the psychic link with the emperor and questioned Mrs. Elko about the prospects of the pretender, Otto, who is Charles's son. Word from Charles came back presently. Otto would never be allowed to live in Austria, but Otto's son would return.

This prediction, made in 1963, came true in 1965. The Habsburg family has since returned to live in Austria, quietly, and without political power. All except one—Otto.

Every researcher in this field welcomes the help of scientifically trained witnesses or subjects because he feels that such persons naturally will be more astute and less emotional observers. And the public is likely to pay greater respect to the word of a trained professional than to that of an ordinary person, although this is prejudicial and based on the old assumption that professional people are by their very nature more reliable than others.

The quality of a person's observations comes from the person's character, not his vocation, but it is true that the testimony of professionals is valued highly by parapsychologists because so few professionals have the integrity and *courage* to speak up when something out of the ordinary happens to them. The scientific community today, more than ever, frowns on the unorthodox, despite vast strides made in areas where very little is known, for example, space research. For a professional highly regarded in his community there are very real dangers, or at least disadvantages, in engaging in research along unorthodox lines. It is therefore with genuine regret, but also prudence, that I withhold the name and address of my next subject.

Dr. N. was a medical doctor when I met him, a general practitioner lately engaged also in psychiatric work, living in a large city in California. He was in good health, and had an excellent professional record.

What prompted him to get in touch with me to discuss his experiences was a request in one of my books for people with ESP to come forward and help me explore this realm further.

In August 1966, I first learned of the doctor's amazing psychic experiences, experiences that, I hasten to add, he has always tried to explain on purely rational and scientific grounds, only to discover that the orthodox scientific approach offered no satisfactory explanation. Until we met, the doctor had never discussed his experiences seriously with anyone.

We met in the cocktail lounge of the Hotel St. Francis in San Francisco. The doctor had decided to meet me "on neutral grounds," in a location where nobody was likely to recognize either of us. With the distant cocktail music as background, we discussed his case.

Evidently psychic abilities had come to the doctor through his family. His grandmother could move a heavy piano merely by touching it lightly. This is a natural force known to parapsychologists as the same energy utilized in table-tipping and not necessarily a proof of the existence of spirits.

His mother was gifted with clairvoyance to such an extent that "she could not walk down the street without people thronging around her, asking her to tell their future." It became such a bother that she wanted nothing to do with her unexpected talent.

At the age of five, the doctor and his twin brother were visiting a neighbor's house. The neighbors had a grand piano. The young boy was drawn to the piano, although he had never played one and knew nothing whatever about music. Before he knew it, his hands were on the keyboard and playing a flawless rendition of "America the Beautiful."

More inexplicable events occurred in the year that followed this incident. His parents did not have a piano, so the boy became almost a plague to the neighbors, driven by a strange compulsion to play the instrument.

"Even today," the doctor said lightly, "I can play by ear music which is commonly mistaken for Bach or Italian Baroque. I do not read music, have never studied it, and have no explanation to offer as to where this strange talent comes from."

When the neighbors finally refused to let the boy use their piano, he flew into a rage—something the quiet, shy boy would not normally do—and cut one leg off the piano in revenge!

Between his sixth year and his teens, his psychic talent lay dormant, then returned in full force. Again the piano became an obsession, and now the young man could hear harpsichord music in his mind and he would visualize a pair of hands on the keyboard of the ancient instrument. Many times he would be half-asleep, and yet his hands were playing entire concert pieces, as if someone were directing them.

On one occasion he entered a church and suddenly found himself playing the organ, although he had never done so before. Despite the numerous stops and several keyboards, the youngster deftly found his way around the organ to the amazement of the organist, who insisted the piece he had just heard was Bach—although he could not identify it by name!

The boy explained politely that he had never studied music and knew nothing about Bach. The organist got very angry and called him a liar.

Soon he discovered that there was a telepathic tie between himself and his identical twin brother. On several occasions they wrote each other letters, the letters crossed in the mail and, upon comparing them later, they found they had written almost identical letters.

On one occasion the young man grabbed his mother's arm and insisted they leave a friend's house immediately because his brother was going to telephone from three thousand miles away. At the very instant they opened their front door, the phone started to ring, and sure enough, it was the brother.

Once, the doctor was to pick up a younger brother and drive him to meet their parents in Berkeley, California. They were late, and their parents had gone out to dinner. Without a moment's hesitation, the doctor drove on, like a homing pigeon making for the coop. At a street intersection in San Francisco, he caught up with his parents' car. How? He had no idea. He just followed his inner promptings and drove on.

"You realize the statistical odds against such a thing happening," the doctor said, "but I have found my brother on other occasions purely by instinct, without conscious knowledge where he might be. I used to blame this strange ability on the fact that my twin and I have similar IQs, similar thoughts and habits, but I am not so sure of this explanation any longer. I think it is something else."

Our conversation now veered to predictions and premonitions. Evidently the doctor had a well-developed second sight but was hesitant to talk about it to strangers for fear of being ridiculed.

"There was a certain dream," he began. "It happened to me in 1955 and was in three parts. I dreamt it in something like 3D and Technicolor—if that is the word."

"What was remarkable about the dream?" I asked.

"In the first part I visualized a car accident in which I was to be involved. In the second part I saw an episode dealing with Mexicans and involving a dog in which my life would be in danger, and in the third part I was at Stanford University, and I saw some vapor trails in the air left by large bombers and then I saw a mushroom cloud over the city. . . ."

"What about the car accident? Let us take this part first."

"I saw distinctly that it was my car going up an incline on Highway 99 past Bakersfield. I knew the time and the make of the car ahead of me—the sun was just setting, but I did not know when, what day this would occur. I was so strongly impressed by the dream that I reported it to my aunt and uncle in complete detail."

In the morning, the doctor left his relatives and drove toward Los Angeles. He had put the dream out of his mind, to concentrate on the road. But as the sun began to set, there was an accident, just as he had seen it in his dream.

"The strange thing is," the doctor commented, "that I could not have prevented it even if I had wanted to. The car in front of me had stopped to make a turn. Because it was on a hill, the driver had not put on his brake lights and was riding the clutch. There was no warning, and the sun was in my eyes, and me going in his lane at sixty miles an hour—I smacked right into him. Luckily, nobody got hurt."

"What about the other two parts of your dream in 1955?"

"I found this out only recently. In medical school I had a dog that bit a Mexican boy. The family was going to find out who owned the dog and 'get him.' But they did not succeed, and instead did away with the dog. Thus I was saved from possible danger at the hands of the angry parents of the boy."

"What about the third part of your dream?"

The doctor's face became grim. "It has not happened as yet," he said slowly, "and I keep hoping it never will. But. . . ."

There was a moment of silence, punctured only by occasional noises from the bar.

We left the subject for a moment and talked about the practical applications of ESP in the doctor's medical treatments. Many times he has had definite feelings about the nature or area of a patient's illness at the first meeting and, upon examination, has discovered that his intuitive impression was entirely correct. He has tried, in vain, to explain these things to himself as due to some slight clue from the patient, but on many occasions there simply was no clue. Now he accepts this strange gift as an invaluable aid in his diagnostic work.

"When I was an intern I used to bet the resident on diagnosis, and when I won six straight cases, he stopped betting. There were so many cases it was almost routine, but I recall one particular case of a patient being taken to surgery for cancer of the liver, and I told the patient, 'You don't have to worry about cancer of the liver. You haven't got it. You have an amoebic abscess,' and it turned out just as I had said it would."

Shades of Edgar Cayce, I thought. Was this not a man who did many of the things the great seer of Virginia Beach had done—with the additional advantage of being a medical man *himself*?

The doctor is not superstitious; he believes only that which he can see or test for himself. But neither is he prejudiced against that which is unusual. He cannot make his psychic sense work whenever he wants it to. He does not wait for it, but when it does come to him, he welcomes it as a friend.

The doctor was curious about these influences, both the force that led him to the piano and the medical knowledge he could not have logically.

For a number of years before we met, he had felt the "presence" of two people around him from time to time. He wondered if this was just his imagination, for he could neither see nor hear these personalities and yet they were in his consciousness.

The one that drove him to the piano was a girl of about sixteen. One day he discovered that his grandmother, who had died long before he was born, had been a devoted pianist and had forced her daughter—his mother—to learn to play the piano against her will. In fact, one of the reasons the doctor did not have a piano at home when he was young was his mother's abhorrence of the instrument. She did not want her son to suffer from the ivory-toothed monster the way she had!

The doctor wonders if it is not this grandmother who works through him, if he has, as he suspects, psychic powers.

As for the medical knowledge, and especially his remarkable power of diagnosis, he "feels" the influence of a British doctor around him. This man, whose name he knows, died, he thinks, in Burma in 1941. Cut off before his time, the dead doctor may be expressing himself through Dr. N.

World predictions have fascinated many gifted with a sixth sense. Some will stick their necks out and make exact predictions about things they feel will happen in a given time period. It is perhaps a backhanded solace that a portion of these predictions—many of them dire—never materialize. But one never knows which ones will and which ones won't.

CHAPTER 4

Premonitions:
Warning Prophecies

There are two kinds of prophecies: those that predict events that will surely occur, and those that foretell of events that *may* occur but that are not yet inevitable. Events described under the latter type of prophecy may be altered or even avoided if mankind heeds the warnings and takes action to change the course of the future. Parapsychologists call these prophecies premonitions—warning prophecies.

Unfortunately it is not always clear as to whether a prophecy is inescapable, but when determined people believe that there is a chance to save the world from impending doom, when people refuse to simply accept the terrible future that fate seems to have in store, when they fight back in whatever way they know how, they may indeed find that they are able to alter future events and avoid the realization of a dire, perhaps life-threatening, prophecy.

The word *premonition* means to "suspect ahead of time" and applies to the entire range of foreknowledge of impending events, from a vague feeling of doom or discomfort to a precise knowledge of a future event. Although most premonitions deal with unpleasant occurrences, this is not necessarily characteristic of the process itself. What is required, however, is some kind of emotional color to the event. It so happens that the negative, destructive emotion is usually stronger and thus makes a stronger imprint on the unconscious mind than the happy event.

Premonitions differ from predictions in many ways. Premonitory experiences are largely feeling, and even though they may contain verbal messages, some emotionalism, the atmosphere of feeling, is always present. Not so with predictions, most of which are made "in cold blood," often at will by trained psychics. Thus we can say that most premonitions are *emotional* forms of ESP while predictions are essentially *intellectual* attempts to pierce the veil of future events.

Premonitions can come to almost anyone. They are unexpected and uncontrollable, often unwanted and sometimes upsetting. Predictions, on the other hand, can be pleasant experiences, and they can be suppressed if the moment is not right. Even though both extrasensory experiences derive from the same source—that is, the psyche of the person having the experience—they seem to be manifest at different levels of consciousness or perhaps at different depths of the same level. Occasionally, the borderline between the two forms of ESP phenomena disappears and a person may experience both forms of paranormal knowledge at the same time.

It is also a moot question whether a psychic *predicts* out of his own unconscious knowledge or through the intermediary of a "spirit force." But there can be no doubt that the source of *premonitions* is always firmly rooted in the individual. If an outside entity is responsible for the premonitory knowledge, the subject is not aware of it at the time.

Some events apparently are so powerful, so loaded with emotional impact, that their approach impresses itself on more than one person. Many catastrophes have been felt ahead of time by a number of people. Frequently such premonitions come to a person during the dream state, since the individual is then more open to messages on the unconscious level, the conscious mind being temporarily disconnected.

Don't sell dreams short—the "gypsy dream interpreters" and "ancient Egyptian dream books" notwithstanding. A dream is not an event, it is a state of being, almost as important to a person's consciousness as the waking state. In fact, I feel that the dreaming and waking states are counterparts, the two halves of the whole. Psychiatrists have long recognized this fact and make good use of dreams for interpretation and analysis of their subjects. In the same manner, some dreams (but by no means all) convey material contained in neither the conscious nor the unconscious mind of the subject. This material, clearly received from outside the personality, may contain information not yet passed into objective reality. If this material later becomes part of the conscious experience of the individual (or of those to whom the material applies), we speak of premonitions come true.

The unconscious is a curious element. Depending entirely on the individual, his emotional makeup, background, health, accumulated knowledge, it can be a very efficient clearinghouse of information or a foggy, symbol-shrouded chamber of horrors.

Just as the skill of the psychoanalyst unknots the weavings of the unconscious to extricate the hard-core facts, so the parapsychologist unravels the yarns of symbolism, fantasy, dream fulfillment, and other interwoven personal elements from the spool of the unconscious to bring into the open the paranormal material, the information pertaining to the future or to places at a distance from the subject. Since we are dealing with people, and human beings differ from person to person, we also find the entire range of communication from the very clear and sharply defined to the murky and greatly obscured, although, in principle, they arrive in the same manner.

Premonitions are as old as mankind. Predictions are perhaps even older than prophecies, which are somewhat more sophisticated in that they require formalizing and verbalization by a gifted individual, whereas predictions can be communicated in the most primitive manner.

The Bible is full of premonitory warnings, sometimes clad in the cloak of religious symbolism, sometimes straightforward.

Joseph began his flight into Egypt when a premonitory dream warned him that the Holy Family was in danger. The highly symbolic dream of Jacob, in which angels ascend and descend the ladder to heaven, also belongs in this category.

It is difficult to determine whether premonitions of disaster, when properly heeded, can avert the impending disaster. The question is academic in most cases, since history bears out the melancholy truth that the majority of people *ignore* the warnings.

But what about those who do not ignore the signs? Do they change their fate by being forewarned? Or, if fate is already set in motion at the time of the premonition, are they merely being advised of what *will* happen to them? I can only conclude that fate is a tricky taskmaster and that in most cases, premonitions of the psychic kind come true and the individual is indeed incapable of escaping his destiny. This even applies to many who were forewarned and tried to escape but could not.

The traditional concept of Death in Samara (about the rich man who had heard that Death was waiting for him in Baghdad and fled to Samara only to discover that Death was already there, waiting for him) seems to hold true in most cases. But there are exceptions, I think, in cases where a man's ability to oppose his fate was being tested: if he judged correctly he was given the key to determine his own fate; if not, it would run its predetermined course.

But personal pride, importance of office or position, or centuries-old taboos constrain many people from acting on a premonition.

One could argue that these were among the reasons the late President Kennedy did nothing about the many messages of warning that were brought to him right up to the eve of the Dallas tragedy. He honestly could not bring himself to believe that the warnings had substance. Even if he had wanted to, the public probably would have considered him weak rather than prudent.

The late Franklin Roosevelt firmly believed in the powers of the psychic world, but only after his death did this become known. But President Kennedy himself had a high degree of ESP, it would appear. On the day of his assassination, he spoke to his wife of the possibility of someone shooting him and repeatedly expressed concern and a general uneasiness over the Dallas trip. All of this is related in most books dealing with the tragedy of November 22, 1963. Unfortunately, Kennedy did not act upon his hunch.

Steward Robb, the greatest authority on the prophecies of Nostradamus, briefly discussed the value of premonitions in an article in the magazine he once edited, *Exploring the Unknown.* The value of proper interpretation of psychic warning is, of course, that to be forewarned is to be forearmed.

Evidently fate wants some of us to escape destruction at certain moments and tips us off so that we can use our ingenuity to survive. It is a little like a tip on the stock market— not everybody gets the signals, but those who do will profit from them.

Steward Robb cites the case of Elizabeth Taylor, who had strong premonitory feelings just before her then-husband, Mike Todd, went on a trip in a private plane. She made only slight mention of those feelings. If she had voiced her fear, would Todd have given in to her and not taken the fatal trip? Having met him once, briefly, I am almost sure the warning would have been to no avail.

After his passing, Todd evidently learned the psychic ropes better. Among the dozen guests at an experimental sitting in the Greenwich Village home of actor Darren McGavin years ago, there was a young man whom I had never seen before. I had brought my friend Ethel Meyers as the medium, and in her trance a personality manifested and immediately picked out the young man for communication. The young man seemed startled, as if he recognized the voice addressing him. None of the others did, however, so I asked that the communicator give his name or initials.

"M.G.," came from Ethel's lips. It made no sense to the others, but after the sitting I questioned the young man about it. He was rather shaken. The voice, he explained, had been that of his late employer, Michael Todd. Mr. Todd's true name was Goldbogen—M.G.

In the communication, Todd expressed regret that he had not heeded his wife's premonition, vague though it had been.

Occasionally premonitory dreams recur—as if to make sure the one who is to be warned really gets the message.

In the *Journal of the Society for Psychical Research,* Steward Robb reports on the well-known case of the Honorable J. O'Connor, who had booked passage on the maiden voyage of the *Titanic.* Ten days before departure, he dreamed he saw the ship floating in the sea and passengers swimming around it. The next night, he had the same dream again. He spoke of his dream to his family, then canceled his trip.

The Daily American of West Frankfort, Illinois, and *Fate* magazine published accounts of a coal miner named Roscoe Harris, who had a premonitory dream in which he clearly saw an accident involving the third cage of the mine where he worked—he saw the cage fall and kill twenty-nine people.

The next morning he arrived at the mine just as the cage, with twenty-five aboard, was about to descend. His shouting caused the superintendent to halt the cage. After hearing of the dream, the superintendent had chains placed around the cage as a precautionary measure.

The cage was ready to descend again, this time with twenty-nine men, since four more miners had arrived in the meantime. During the descent, the accident happened exactly as Harris had seen it in his dream but because of the chains, nobody was hurt. It was then that the superintendent admitted that he had had the same dream the night before the accident!

Ian Stephens, then a professor at King's College, Cambridge, England, had a waking vision of the school chapel, scaffolded for repairs at the time, projected onto the door of his room. In his vision, the body of a man was swinging from the scaffolding, and the word *dean* impressed itself in his mind.

He rushed outside to satisfy himself that no body was hanging from the scaffolding. Just then he ran into a fellow scholar to whom he reported the details of his vision. Four days later, the dean of the college was found dead at the foot of the scaffold. He had not hanged himself but had thrown himself to his death. This case was reported by both the *Psychic News* and the British weekly *Weekend*.

Another British case concerns the crash of a British airplane in the summer of 1966 at Ljubljana, Yugoslavia, in which ninety-seven people were killed. This was a special holiday excursion plane. One of the passengers, Mrs. Ronald Alexander, told a neighbor she wished she and her husband were not going on the trip, and left explicit instructions what to do if she should not return. She and her husband were among the victims.

Not all premonitions deal with disaster. Linda Latz of California comes from a family in which ESP experiences run in the female line. Her mother has frequently dreamed of events before they happened.

In 1938, Linda was on a ship en route from San Francisco through the Panama Canal to New York City. Linda had no specific plans for the various shore points along the route, nor any intention of going beyond New York. While aboard ship, her mother communicated to Linda a dream she had had, in which she saw Linda visiting a rum factory and then going to London.

To her surprise, Linda was invited to visit a rum factory at Havana, and after debarking at New York and staying there for two weeks, she did decide to visit London.

In 1953 Linda's mother was bedridden with arthritis and her father had to go to the hospital for an examination. Although nothing serious was found, he contracted pneumonia and had to stay in the hospital. The doctors did not think it was serious and so informed the family. Linda developed a routine of visiting with her mother in the morning and with her father in the afternoon. On the ninth day after her father had gone to the hospital, her mother insisted that she change her routine and go and see her father in the morning, immediately, in fact. Linda agreed. She found her father in good spirits, stayed for an hour, and went home. A short time later the phone rang. Her father had taken a sudden turn for the worse. By the time Linda got to the hospital he had passed on.

"He called me, for he wanted to sit up," the nurse explained, "and then his head fell back on the pillow and he was gone."

When Linda brought the sad news to her mother, she found her mother already expecting it. She told her daughter of a dream she had had the night before—the dream that made her insist Linda go to see her father first thing in the morning. In the dream she and her husband were occupying berths in a Pullman car. Her husband suddenly said, "I just wanted to say goodbye," and his head fell back on the pillow.

Premonitions come to people who are completely disinterested in anything of this kind as often as to those already familiar with the occult. Psychic talent makes no distinctions between persons or backgrounds.

Lucy K. was born in 1911 in a small town in Kentucky. After graduating from a Florida university, she taught school for twenty years, eventually becoming a school principal. Because of her standing in her community, I am omitting her name, which, however, along with all other names of the witnesses here mentioned, is in my possession. Mrs. K. is well-liked and a confidante of many troubled souls. As she put it, "even dogs like me." Married in 1936, she had two sons.

As long as she can remember, she has been psychic. Many times she knows what a person is about to say, or she answers a question not yet put to her.

On July 5, 1942, she had a premonitory dream that saddened her very much. Her younger son, C., had had an accident, and she saw her neighbors pass by in a red truck and look significantly toward her house. She clearly recognized the woman sitting in the truck as a Mrs. I. The following day, the accident happened, and the truck passed her house precisely as it had in her dream.

On December 10, 1956, she went to school as usual. She found herself talking to one of the school employees, wondering why her elder son had not come home the night before.

"I have a feeling he is dead," she said simply, to the horror of the young woman. But she went on to her classes. A little later, there was a phone call. Her son had had a fatal accident that morning at 7:30 A.M.

In January 1960, Mrs. K. awakened her husband one morning at 5:30 A.M. to tell him that her sister-in-law was dead. This was later confirmed; the dying woman's last words had been the names of Mr. and Mrs. K. This of course is ESP over a distance rather than pure premonition; but two nights *before* her neighbor died, Mrs. K. saw her standing at the foot of her bed, wearing a long white dress, and knew the neighbor would die soon.

Around Thanksgiving 1966, as Mrs. K. was walking down the back steps of the schoolhouse, the thought came to her that nothing much had happened in their little community of late. Immediately a terrible dread filled her and she knew bad tidings lay ahead. The following day her next-door neighbor died, two days later another friend passed away suddenly, and still another woman friendly to her was murdered—all three events happened within one week.

T. F. Tweedle of California had his first psychic experience while he was serving with the Gordon Highlanders during World War I. His outfit was in the middle of an attack, with enemy machine-gun fire all around them. He was about to go forward with the others in a frontal attack and wondered if he'd live through it. Suddenly, he *knew* he would not be killed, he would not be wounded, but *something* would happen to him. Reassured by this, he went "over the top," as he put it, and the premonition turned out to be only too true. He was not killed, he was not wounded, but something did happen to him: he was gassed.

In another action, Mr. Tweedle found himself shouting at his "number two" at the machine gun, "Take over the gun as soon as I am wounded." He wondered what had possessed him to say this, but half an hour later he knew. He was wounded and on his way to the hospital.

When I was in Hollywood in 1966 to do a number of radio and television shows, I met a lady named Virginia White via the telephone. She was one of the more interesting callers on programs such as Ron McCoy's show, where listeners got on the air by calling in questions to the guest or host.

Mrs. White had had psychic experiences for many years and does not mind talking about them. Raised by her grandparents, she knows only that her mother was a French actress and her father, whom she hardly knew, a traveling musician. She went to high school, graduated in 1938, and married four years later. She and her husband went to California; he worked in the motion picture industry and died in 1964. They shared a certain understanding of psychic matters and often had similar dreams. After his passing she says she saw him a number of times, especially when she was ill and in need of help.

In 1955 Mrs. White was working for the William Stevens Company in Los Angeles. Since her home was only a block from her place of work, it was her custom to go home for lunch to spend some time with her husband. One day as she was returning to her job around 1:00 P.M., she was waiting for the green light at the intersection of Santa Monica Boulevard and Las Palmas Avenue. The light changed and, as she started to cross, an apparition appeared; one of the shipping clerks at the office was lying in the street before her, so close that she would have had to step over him to cross the street. The next moment the crumpled figure was gone. Already late, she hurried on to work. As she explained her tardiness to her superior, a piercing scream filled the air. It was from the back of the plant. There, lying on the pavement, was the crumpled figure of the shipping clerk she had seen in her vision. He had been climbing a ladder to the roof, was momentarily distracted by someone below, turned around and fell. He did not die, but it was a close call.

In this case the premonition came as a definite image rather than a vague feeling of impending disaster. Telepathy is not a possible explanation here, since the accident occurred after the vision had been observed. It would appear to be premonitory clairvoyance on the part of Mrs. White, who simply foresaw what would happen in her life within the next hour or so, and the harrowing experience of witnessing a near-fatal accident certainly was a major event to her.

Premonitions come to the young as well as to the old; in fact, many excellent mediums show promise at an early age. Mrs. Patricia G. K. of Vancouver, Washington, is now twenty-nine-years old. When she was fifteen, she had an experience that has remained with her ever since.

It was afternoon and she was preparing for a performance

of the high school chorus that evening. Her boyfriend and another friend were to call for her and another girl and take them to the concert. While she was waiting for the hours to pass, she lapsed into a state between sleep and wakefulness, which was suddenly interrupted by a vision of her boyfriend leaning across the front end of his car, his head in his hands, sobbing "Oh, my God . . . oh, my God!" over and over. There was blood all over the front fender of the car.

An hour later, the other girl telephoned. The boys would not be able to pick her up, after all. There had been an accident. The car struck and killed an old woman who was crossing a dark street in the middle of the block. She described the scene and mentioned that the front fender was covered with blood.

Later, when she had calmed down, Patricia G. K. was able to "compare notes." Everything happened the way she had foreseen it, except that the other boy had been driving.

Elizabeth Vignola, a lady of more than ninety years, lived quietly in Los Angeles. Her premonitions dated back a long time. In 1926, for example, she and her husband were sitting on a wooden staircase in Coney Island, New York. An uneasy feeling made her move away from the spot, much to her husband's annoyance. But a week later, the staircase collapsed, injuring many persons.

Standing at a corner on Fulton Street in New York where the elevated came around a sharp curve, she found herself wondering about an accident at that spot. The following week, a train was derailed at the spot under which she had stood.

Like so many others, Mrs. Vignola had a Kennedy premonition. Hers happened in the spring of 1963, and she confided her dream to several people, who promptly teased her about it. In her dream she saw herself walking beside the president through a large hall. She was dressed very elegantly in black.

They walked around a corner and found themselves in front of an empty coffin. At that point, her dream ended.

It did little to salve her conscience when the prediction came true. The melancholy truth is that she could have done nothing about it even if she had tried. Who would listen to the dreams of a little old lady in California—not the Secret Service, that's for sure.

Until we have sufficiently educated the government about precognition and ESP in general, strong impressions concerning the welfare of public figures will not get the notice they sometimes deserve.

"I am twenty-two years old, married, and the mother of a two-year-old daughter," stated Mrs. M. W., when she first contacted me in March 1966. "I'm a senior at Texas A & I, and I have an IQ of approximately 150."

Mrs. W. also had strong psychic talents. What prompted her to contact me on that fateful March 11 was an incident that had occurred that morning.

Her younger sister, who lived with her, had left to take Mr. W. to work in the family car. Then she was to return home and take Mrs. W. to school.

At 7:50 A.M., Mrs. W. suddenly had a strong premonition that her sister was in an accident. At 8:15, she was notified by a mutual friend that her sister had had a collision but was not hurt, although the car was a total loss.

Some psychics are better with deaths, others seem to sense violence, still others are strong on automobile accidents. Mrs. W. was in the last category.

Early in February 1966, she began to have terrible fears that she would not see her mother alive again. Her trepidation increased as the time of her parents' expected visit drew near.

They were due at 3:00 A.M. At 2:00 A.M., Mrs. W. suddenly woke up with the thought that her parents had been in a wreck. With a dreadful certainty, she sat waiting for the phone to ring.

At 3:00 the phone rang. A highway patrolman informed her that her parents had been taken to the hospital. Although seriously injured, her mother survived the crash.

That period was a particularly trying one for the young woman. For some reason, her psychic gifts were heightened during that time. From January 1966 onward, she had a premonition that someone would be involved in a rape, an unwanted pregnancy, and an unsuccessful abortion attempt. She had no idea who the person would be.

In the middle of February, Mrs. W. received a call from her mother. Her sister had been attacked, was pregnant from it, and apparently had taken some birth control pills in a failed attempt to abort the pregnancy—exactly as Mrs. W. had felt in her premonitions.

Mrs. W. evidently had the ability to "tune in" on events at a distance in both time and space. She awoke early one morning with a feeling that something was going to happen. Immediately she focused her "third eye" on the feeling to see if she could narrow it down from this broad generality.

"Someone is about to die; it is someone important." At this point her husband, who was at first alarmed, decided to go back to sleep, while Mrs. W. continued her psychic "fine-tuning." Instantly her sixth sense told her, "It's an important statesman."

As an ardent conservative, Mrs. W. wondered if it meant Goldwater. Then the inner voice said, "A person important to the nation, but not to you." At that point the psychic lady shrugged and said aloud, "Oh, well, it doesn't matter; he just died."

The next day her husband checked the newspapers: Adlai Stevenson had died in London. The time? Allowing for the time difference, the moment Mrs. W. had felt it.

Mrs. W. had been psychic since her early teens, as was her mother before her. At first, this consisted only of such things as knowing who would call, predicting births and deaths, and knowing the answers to school tests before the tests were given.

When she reached fourteen, her psychic energy was so strong that objects moved about by their own volition in her presence, a fact her mother attested to. During the poltergeist stage of her youth, Mrs. W. was never alarmed by the phenomena but took them naturally.

Not many people in her hometown would believe that she possessed paranormal faculties, and as a consequence, Mrs. W. had not discussed these matters with outsiders. Although she was far from ashamed or worried about her psychic experiences, she asked me to withhold her name and address because of her interest in politics; she did not want to be prejudged because of what to some people sounds far-out or even unnatural.

Of mixed Anglo-Saxon, French, German, and Indian background, Mrs. W. came from an old East Texas family. Psychic ability had been in the family for several generations; her mother was psychic, her maternal grandfather won fame as a dowser, and her great-grandmother was a schoolteacher, a strict Methodist, and a trance medium, all in one. Among the premonitory visions of Mrs. W.'s mother was one concerning the car in which she had a terrible accident en route to her daughter's house. She knew she would get hurt in that car the first time she laid eyes on it—and yet she went.

"My 'hunches' become stronger as I grow older," explained Margaret Casey, of St. Louis, another of the many thousands of Americans who have frequent premonitions of impending events.

Mrs. Casey's father was driving to Arkansas to visit his father in the hospital, and he asked her to drive down with him. She agreed to go. She would have to take her baby along because her husband would be at work. Two days before the trip—in October 1965—she had such a strong premonition about a wreck that she decided not to accompany her father on his trip. He scoffed at her fears and went alone. On the way back, his car skidded and was hit on the right side by an oncoming car. If Mrs. Casey had gone along, her baby would most likely have been in the backseat on the right side!

On December 27, 1965, the Caseys left Texas to move to St. Louis. They said their good-byes to all their friends, except for one family, very close and dear to them, who were out of town at the time of their departure. When they returned, they expressed regret at having been away from home to Mrs. Casey's mother, who conveyed their feelings to her daughter, now settled in St. Louis.

Instead of being pleased at such expression of concern, Mrs. Casey became terribly depressed. On February 17, 1966, she had a dream in which she clearly saw the wife and the daughter of that family, but not the husband. Moreover, the two women were wearing long black dresses and black veils, and they were crying.

The next morning she felt sure that something was wrong with the husband, and wanted to phone her mother in Houston to warn him. But Mrs. Casey had been ridiculed so often for her psychic impulses that she decided to forget it, ascribing it all to a "bad dream."

Two days later, on February 20, her mother telephoned. The husband in her friend's family, a man of forty-one in excellent physical condition, who had only recently seen his doctor, had dropped dead.

Mrs. Casey did not know why she had these premonitory flashes; she accepted them as part of her makeup and tried to put them to good use.

Sometimes it takes a healthy sense of humor to live with the supernormal. William B. Lowe is a young man who has experiences that neither frighten nor mystify him, for he realizes that he is mediumistic. He has heard his name called many times in an empty house and has been made aware of a presence anxious to communicate in what he knew was an empty room.

"I seem to be able to sense when something is going to happen," he explains. "But I believe myself to be normal. I am thirty-five years old and have seven daughters and a good job. With seven girls you *need* a good job."

Some time ago, as he was getting into a car with a group of friends, an inner voice told him, "Don't go; there is going to be an accident."

He did not wish to appear odd, so he went. There was an accident and the car was demolished, but he was not hurt.

"It wasn't an actual voice I heard," he explained, "more or less words that formed in my mind."

Dave Hart has had a number of ESP experiences, but it is his girlfriend, Donna Roden, who is the central character of the following experience. The story was reported at the time it happened in the *Great Falls Tribune*.

On November 22, 1963, at noon sharp, the girl, a freshman at Dawson County Junior College, was coming out of class when she was seized with a psychic impression.

"The president is dead," she said for all around her to hear.

Nothing had as yet been announced. On rechecking the time, it appeared that her impression was simultaneous with the event transpiring in Dallas, Texas, while she was in the heart of Montana.

Evelyn I. is a secretary at a major western hospital. She has been psychic for as long as she can remember. Many times she knows of events before they occur, and it causes her panic—not because extrasensory perception is frightening to her but because she feels so helpless at not being able to stop the events she has envisioned.

She knows which patient will live and which will die; she was correct in so many cases that she felt she could no longer have patients sign "their own death certificates" when signing routine releases for hospital treatment; she asked to be relieved of this phase of her duties, although she realized it would change nothing as far as fate was concerned.

Because of her medical training and generally calm attitude toward death, she wanted to study in order to develop her psychic talents. No matter what kind of psychic divination she attempts, the results are the same: evidential. She realizes that reading cards, coffee grounds, and tea leaves, and staring into a crystal ball are all the same form of tapping the unconscious and that the knowledge comes from the psychic reservoir of the subject, not from the objects used to induce the psychic state!

Late in 1965 she predicted that the two children of a friend would be involved with a third child in a great tragedy. Four days later, the three children were playing when a heavy scaffold collapsed and killed the third child in the presence of her friend's two children.

A sudden flash, a waking vision, showed her a friend who lived some distance from her; she felt that this friend would burn her right arm. She immediately wrote to her friend, warning her to take care, but the warning came too late. The accident had taken place at the exact moment that Evelyn saw it happen. Moreover, the injured woman had turned to her husband at that time, saying she wanted to call Evelyn.

There is no inherent difference between premonitions felt ahead of time and those events happening simultaneously but out of sight of the subject; in fact, there isn't even a basic difference between this type of phenomenon and reading into past events, for the artificial borderline called time does not exist in the psychic dimension. It is only because of our rational concepts that we are more awed by the foretelling of future events than by the recounting of past happenings, perhaps because of the feeling that past events *can* be known to the psychic somehow, while future events cannot be known through either research or trickery.

Like many psychics, Gazelle Soto questioned why she was chosen by fate to know things beforehand. Mrs. Soto contacted me in November 1966. A native of Brooklyn, she lived in Tampa, Florida, most of her years and, for a time, also in Cuba. When she and her husband left Tampa for Havana, they left behind a large circle of relatives and friends and found themselves among strangers. But a job opportunity had taken them to Cuba, and they had to make the best of it.

Mrs. Soto had often dreamed of death and sickness that later came true. So it was with horror that she awoke from a dream one night in which she clearly saw one of their Tampa friends "in a hole in the ground," as she put it. In her dream she had recoiled at this vision, exclaiming that *this* man could not possibly be dead; it was his older brother, who had been very ill, who must have been meant!

She was so upset over the dream that she wrote to her mother in Tampa asking her to find out how the two brothers were getting along. The answer came by return mail. The younger brother had passed on three days earlier from pneumonia. The other brother lived to be ninety.

In 1934, while Mrs. Soto was living in Tampa, she became friendly with a family who lived next door. The youngest child of that family was a girl of seven. In a dream one night, Mrs. Soto "saw" the girl laid out dead on the porch of the house, and in the dream she felt terribly sad about it all. The next morning she reported her dream to her mother, who told her to forget it and to dream something pleasant for a change.

Three months passed, and Mrs. Soto got to know the little girl better. One morning, the child fell ill. What was diagnosed at first as measles turned out to be diphtheria, and the child got worse. Now the dream returned to haunt Mrs. Soto and she wondered whether she should tell the child's mother about the danger she foresaw for the girl. However, she just couldn't do it. One morning the mother came to her in tears asking for help, and it was then that Mrs. Soto suggested they bring in a specialist. But it was too late. The girl died that night and when Mrs. Soto saw her laid out on the porch, she realized that her dream had shown her the truth in every detail, three months before!

But Mrs. Soto's premonitions did not always concern other people. While she was visiting her family in Tampa, a vision appeared on the wall of her bedroom in which the symbolic figure of Death stood beside her, and she heard a voice telling her that she would be very ill but would not die.

Again she confided in her mother, but her mother had no belief in such things. A month after the vision, back in Havana, Mrs. Soto fell seriously ill from an infection and almost died. Her father, a physician, managed to save her life after a struggle.

Following her mother's admonition to dream something pleasant for a change, Mrs. Soto, unwittingly of course, did just that in the 1930s. Her sister wanted very much to visit her in Havana but could not afford the trip. Mrs. Soto wanted to help her but did not have the money either. This was during the Depression, when almost everyone was poor.

Three days before Cuba's national lottery took place that year, Mrs. Soto had a strange dream. She and her sister were in a swimming pool filled with small ducks. The picture was unusually clear. Upon awakening, she consulted a dream book. She turned to the page listing numbers for certain symbols or pictures people experience in dreams. I have never felt that these explanations have any relation to reality, but evidently this case was an exception.

"Ducks" was number 22 in the book, and Mrs. Soto promptly sent a dollar to her mother in Florida to play in the lottery, as the odds in Florida were higher than in Havana. To everybody's amazement but hers, 22 was the winning number and paid off sufficiently to allow the two sisters to be reunited.

Still another premonitory feeling saved her from danger and possible injury. Years before her marriage she had a Saturday night date to go dancing, but all that day she had an uneasy feeling that someone would rob her. She followed her premonition and put only small change, cosmetics, and her house keys into her purse that night.

Her escort brought her home about 1:30 A.M. As he was putting his car into the garage, she was momentarily left alone in the dark. Looking for her keys, she put the purse on the banister of the house when a strange man suddenly appeared out of the night. He asked her for directions to a nearby street, moving closer to her all the time. Thinking quickly, she pointed to the garage and suggested he ask her boyfriend. Instead, the man leaped up, grabbed the purse, and ran. Had there been a lot of money in the purse, she probably would not have given it up so easily, but her premonition again proved the old adage that forewarned is forearmed.

Occasionally, a premonition can prevent the worst but will not change the entire course of events. A good example is the case of Mrs. Nellie Shultz, a Mirada, California, housewife who has known for many years that she is psychic.

On one occasion she told her truck-driver husband that she had just had a vision concerning him.

"Look for a woman pulling out in front of you," she said. "This will be on a highway, either going into or coming out of a small town. If you're not careful, you will hit her and send her car around a lamppost on a corner near a fireplug."

The husband nodded politely and promised to be careful, the way husbands do.

The feeling of impending danger persisted in Mrs. Shultz. Three months later, her husband was driving out of a small town when suddenly a woman driver pulled out ahead of him. Simultaneously, his wife's warning came back to him. The woman braked suddenly, but he was able to turn his truck in time and thus hit only her left bumper. If he had hit her head-on, she would have been "wrapped around a lamppost" at the corner.

Mr. Shultz has a great deal more respect for his wife's psychic impressions these days. This was not always so. A few years ago, they were on their way to visit a brother of Mr. Shultz's. Hardly had they left town when Mrs. Shultz told her husband that his brother would not be at home. Ignoring her Mr. Shultz drove on. To his consternation, she was soon proved right. Demanding an explanation for her inside knowledge, he did not get one, for Mrs. Shultz did not know herself.

Mrs. Shultz fell asleep as they were driving back to Los Angeles. Suddenly she was startled awake by a strange sound in the car. Her husband assured her it was nothing more than a hole in the manifold caused by a rock they had driven over, and said not to worry. A few miles farther, just as they were going up an incline, Mrs. Shultz had a vision of their car on fire. Her husband thought this ridiculous, and her insistence angered him.

Finally her hysterics forced him to stop the car. They jumped out, and Mr. Shultz started to look the car over. As he opened the hood, flames shot up. But because they had discovered the problem at this point, the fire was brought under control and they were able to fix the car enough to continue.

Mr. Shultz thought they would not be able to make it to a nearby city, where he had family. To his surprise, Mrs. Shultz assured him they would, but barely. The car limped along and finally groaned to a stop just within the city limits, as predicted!

One sometimes hears—from critics who really do not know the subject fully—that psychic people are lacking in other areas of their personalities and make up for this by trying to be "special" or different. This does hold true in a number of cases, but, because they are poor examples, I generally exclude such subjects from my research. The majority of people I have met with ESP powers are well-adjusted individuals to whom the sixth sense is truly an extra faculty, not wished for, not expected— but usually welcome. A good example of this healthy attitude is Mrs. Walt Torrence, of California.

"I don't know if what I have is a good thing, or an evil thing, but I know it is real. I keep telling myself it can't be bad because after all I am very fortunate in life. I have a lovely family—four children. The children as well as my husband and myself are all blessed with good health and good looks. We all work hard, live comfortably, and most of all, we all *love*—everything completely. The world—the universe—all people, flowers, animals, and even criminals and sinners. In other words, we are content, happy, and what anyone would be proud to be themselves."

These are certainly the sentiments of a well-adjusted individual.

In December 1965 Mrs. Torrence and her husband were watching television when she had a flash-like waking vision, accompanied by "sound effects," so to speak. In it a friend by the name of Ted Brasket, an iron worker, was speeding in his Mustang and suddenly there were two sharp noises, which sounded to Mrs. Torrence like blowouts. A second later she saw her friend rolling down a hill and assumed he was dead.

Greatly shaken, she reported the scene to her husband. He tried to calm her, but to no avail. Sleep would not come, and around midnight Mrs. Torrence decided to telephone close friends of Brasket's to find out if they had heard anything about him. The friends had not heard anything from or about Mr. Brasket, and what on earth made her call about it at this hour? She reported her psychic experience to them, fervently hoping that she was wrong.

But she wasn't. Thirty-six hours later and three hundred miles away, Ted Brasket and a friend, Jim Rose, were caught speeding. A policeman gave chase and stopped them. What happened then is a matter of some dispute. The policeman claimed that his gun went off accidentally. At any rate, he fired *two shots,* one killing Mr. Rose, the other injuring Mr. Brasket in the leg, causing him to roll down a hill.

The ties between twins, especially identical twins, can be extraordinarily strong. This is not only on the physical level— one twin feeling pain where the other does, for example—but is even more pronounced on the etheric level.

A case in point happened at Christmas 1952 during the Korean War. Sergeant Martin Hochenberger of Queens, New York, wrote to his mother on December 24, 1952, that he had had a premonition of his impending death. He felt he would not return from night patrol that evening. The letter did not reach his mother until several days later. On December 25, the sergeant's twin sister Lillian had a strong premonitory feeling that something would happen to her brother. On January 2, 1953, the family was notified that the young man had been killed while on night patrol Christmas Eve.

Premonitions can also *save* lives, of course. According to an Associated Press release of July 29, 1963, Royce Atwood Wight was having a nap in a cottage in Miami, Florida. In his dream state, he had a strong premonition of trouble, woke up, and rushed out of the room. A few seconds later, a heavy slab of concrete from a nearby building site crashed through the roof of the room.

A similar example is the experience of Mrs. Mildred Liebowitz of Brooklyn, New York. While still living in her mother's house, she had a radio on a shelf over her bed. While trying to fall asleep one night, Mrs. Liebowitz's mother had a vision of her daughter entwining her arm in the radio cord and pulling the heavy radio down on her head, killing her instantly. The mother ran into her daughter's room, and sure enough, the girl's arm was already entwined in the cord. One more move would have sent the radio crashing down on her head.

The now defunct *New York Journal-American*, dateline January 17, 1962, reported the eerie premonition of a woman named Pauline Elsasser, who was about to drive to Florida with her husband. She told her son that she did not want to go because something was going to happen. But the plans had been made, and so they went. On a clear day, and on a road free of traffic, the car slammed into a bridge wall near Marion, South Carolina, killing all occupants.

Alice Hille is a secretary. In April 1966, she dreamed of a fire and saw a priest at the scene. The following afternoon, the apartment of a friend caught fire from a blaze in an adjoining church.

Richard Parkinson of Long Island, New York, had had repeated visions of a fire involving his family; specifically, he knew that his daughter-in-law and a grandchild would die in a fire. On February 17, 1962, the *New York News* reported the death in a flash fire of Mrs. Richard Parkinson, Jr., and her two-year-old daughter Georgia Lisa. The father-in-law had to be restrained from dashing into the burning building.

Europeans are not so matter-of-fact about the uncanny as Americans or at least Anglo-Saxons are. Perhaps this is a result of continued repression of unorthodox experiences by society and church, or perhaps the rising tide of materialism. When continental Europeans do speak of their psychic adventures, it is only after studious evaluation of the inquirer's intentions.

Mrs. Alice Urbach lived in New York City. Her father was a respected citizen in Vienna. She had a number of psychic experiences and premonitions. In 1918, for instance, she was visiting the apartment of a friend, the wife of a Dr. Hans Kruger. As she turned to leave, she noticed the doctor's name on the door. Suddenly, the name turned into the German words for "never again," and she realized she would not see her friend again. A few days later, the friend died of influenza.

I met Mrs. Margaret McKinley for the first time in the fall of 1966, when I asked her to appear with me on Regis Philbin's KTTV television program. She had lived in a haunted house in San Fernando, and we discussed her eerie experiences in that old house.

Born with a veil in true medium fashion, Mrs. McKinley showed her psychic ability at an early age. At the time her grandmother passed away, the seven-year-old girl saw her death and remarked on it—although three miles away from the house where it took place. Since then she has known of numerous deaths in the family, either just as they happened, or just before, or at a distance.

On Thanksgiving 1961 her in-laws came to visit her and her husband. After her father-in-law left, she turned impulsively to her mother-in-law and said that he would pass away two days later. Since he had not been ill, this was quite a shocking thing to say, but it came true as predicted.

After 1962 her premonitions came mainly in the dream state. On the night of November 21, 1963, she had a horrible nightmare that the president of the United States had been shot. Evidently tuning in on emotionally charged events was part of Mrs. McKinley's psychic gift.

It really beats television, except that you can't tune it *out* quite as easily as *in*! An interesting case involving a premonition in which a deceased person gave warning occurred not long ago. The subject was a very bright and beautiful young girl named Alice Carol M., aged seventeen at the time of the incident. Alice lives with her parents in Brooklyn, New York, and is now a secretary in Manhattan.

Alice has had an unusually fine educational upbringing, speaks French well, and is continuing her studies at one of New York's colleges. She has had psychic experiences since she was twelve, and on several occasions has known when relatives would die or had just died. One of these relatives was her grandmother, who apparently attached herself to the girl as a guide after her passing.

One night Alice dreamed that she went to a store with her parents. She recognized the store as the butcher shop in the neighborhood she had lived in prior to the present address. As they were returning home in the family car, Alice sat in the back instead of the front, where she would normally sit. Suddenly another car hit them and then swerved. It was a grayish car.

All this was shown to her in the dream by her deceased grandmother, who stood to one side of the vision as it unrolled before Alice's eyes like a motion picture.

"See what's going to happen," the grandmother said, and continued, "Now don't let your mommie get hurt. You change places with her, and you won't be hurt badly. But if your mother were hurt, she'd be hurt badly."

With that, the vision vanished.

The following day, everything happened just as it had in the dream. In mounting terror Alice went to the butcher store with her parents. As they were getting back into the car, she decided to heed her grandmother's advice and insisted on getting into the front seat.

Her mother would not let her, and Alice felt she could not tell them of her dream—she would feel foolish if it were all just her imagination. But she insisted on sitting up front with her father, and in the end her mother gave in.

A few moments later, the accident happened, exactly as she had been shown it in her dream. At first, Alice thought she was not hurt. Later she felt pain in her back, and it was found she had received a spinal whiplash. Her mother was shaken up, but not hurt. After Alice returned from the hospital where she had gone for an examination, she told her family about the premonitory dream.

Here, obviously, someone in a position of power—in this case the protecting grandmother—wanted Alice to act in this highly unselfish manner in order to protect her mother. This is just one fascinating example of how the "fate makers" work, or *seem* to work.

PART II

The Prophets Speak: A Survey About the World of the Future

CHAPTER 5

Predictions of Things to Come: Results of a Survey

Back in 1970, I began a systematic project of surveying the field of prophecies and world predictions, which, in addition to allowing me to maintain a record of spontaneous prophecies, would result in a scientific evaluation of the quality of these prophecies and predictions.

The idea was to formulate specific questions about the future of our world, put these questions before a selected group of individuals, record and correlate the results, and come to a composite conclusion as to what the future might hold for us. Naturally, these conclusions could not be verified until the predicted event had either occurred or not, taking into account that specific dates and times are almost impossible to predict accurately, according to most professionals in the field. It has been a quarter of a century since the survey was undertaken. It is now time to evaluate the accuracy and quality of the prophecies made in 1970.

The individuals involved in this survey were selected at random from a pool of psychics, both professionals and amateurs. Their past success in predicting events was the determining factor of their inclusion in this survey. There may, of course, be a great deal of difference in accuracy and in likelihood of occurrence between a prophecy that is made as the result of the psychic's spontaneous vision, urge, dream, or other emotionally tinged event and a prophecy that is consciously and willfully called forth. In order to preserve the statistical integrity of the data, however, a time frame had to be established for collecting all prophecies. In scientific studies, one does not always have the luxury of being able to sit back and wait for evidence to present itself! But if the individuals who had agreed to take part in my project truly had the gift of prophecy, it stands to reason that taking even the less favorable route of requiring "prophecies on demand" would result in a scientifically significant percentage of successful (realized) predictions—albeit with perhaps somewhat less accuracy than if they had been made spontaneously.

Again, I must stress that a survey of this kind cannot be compared in intensity of conviction to spontaneous prophecies coming to the seer unsought, but the individuals surveyed are known psychic individuals and their responses do have a certain weight, if only to show that many predictions never come true as made.

To establish parameters for the survey, I focused on what were (and continue to be) perhaps the most important concerns of the day. These concerns, which are of potentially global consequence, included the following:

- Future wars

- Tomorrow's leaders

- Natural catastrophes

- Racial problems in America

By thus limiting the scope of the survey, it was my intention not only to focus each participant's psychic energies solely on prophecies of vast import, but also to enable me to produce a composite of those statements that might offer a consistently predicted picture of things to come. Now, in 1995, we may review the results of this work and see which prophecies have actually been realized, which may yet occur, and which clearly will not.

The purpose of republishing, with commentaries, prophecies made by a number of people in 1970 (and before) is actually twofold. Since all the individuals who have gone on record with these predictions have established track records of psychic ability, the likelihood that some of the as-yet-unfulfilled prophecies may be realized in the near future must be considered. But that is as far as it goes: *considered*, not necessarily accepted at face value.

The other reason to examine the outcome of these prophecies now, twenty-five years later, is to shed a bit of light on the misconception that prophecies of doom and destruction are somehow more likely to be fulfilled than other, more mundane predictions. Since the majority of the predictions, especially those pertaining to war and disasters, have failed to come true either at the precise time predicted, or even years later, we need to assess our position toward such dire predictions and allow for a much more balanced attitude. Neither ignore prophecies of doom nor swallow them whole.

There is no inherent difference between a prophecy made by an amateur or "minor" prophet of our time and the grand predictions of Biblical prophets, Nostradamus, Malachy, or Edgar Cayce, except in one important respect: the quality of the gift of prophecy. A student playing the piano can produce fairly good music, but nobody will confuse it with the work of Paderewski.

Still, in reviewing this survey, we gain a better handle on the nature of prophecy and the people that possess the gift, as well as an awareness that premonitions do not necessarily seal our fate. A comforting thought to those who scare easily!

The psychics surveyed about tomorrow's world were a cross section of otherwise quite average people. Today's prophets are not mystery-shrouded figures from strange backgrounds, people who can be seen only on special occasions or because of one's own exalted status in life. To be sure, there are some professional seers who like to maintain the mystery of the seers of old. But by and large, psychic people predicting the future today are people like you and me. They may be housewives, secretaries, schoolteachers, or active in any other profession or calling. In that case, their gift of prophecy is merely a sideline, although by no means an unimportant one.

It is difficult to say who are the major prophets and who are the minor ones, because yesterday's beginner may be today's star. The status of psychic people changes in the community of extrasensory perceptors, as it were, according to performance. If they fall below par, word of their failure will soon get around. If, on the other hand, a medium gives some extraordinary proof of his or her ability, word will reach countless people, and the medium will then be beleaguered by thousands who wish to be given private sittings.

Mediumship is a gift that can be improved or neglected. It is not something a person has in the same status and at the same level all his life. This is particularly important to remember when dealing with once-famous mediums who apparently fail today. The power of mediumship goes hand in hand with the general powers of mind and body. It is only human to become weaker as time goes on. Again, this is not an absolute rule. Some very famous mediums have remained active until death. But for anyone evaluating the results of mediumship as it pertains to predicting future events, it is wise to examine the record of each medium at a given time. Chances are that anyone who has consistently performed well is likely to do so on future occasions, although there is no guarantee of a 100 percent performance record. On the other hand, a person who has a long record of foretelling events that have never materialized is not likely to come up with some startling and detailed prognostication. While it is true that the years can either improve or erode the power of mediumship, this is a gradual process and almost never a matter of a sudden jump either up or down.

In listing here the prophets involved in the survey and acquainting readers with their backgrounds, I have followed alphabetical order, to avoid value judgments and professional jealousies. Along with some very major prophets I have included people of great promise. Mediumship is a very democratic craft. Although I have rarely heard one medium say anything really good about another medium, and have frequently met petty jealousy among the professionals in this field, I do not know of instances of serious infighting among mediums, nor have I ever witnessed any really harmful act of one psychic against another. Gossiping seems to be part and parcel of the trade of mediumship.

What is a professional medium? On the surface, of course, a professional medium is anyone with a presumably genuine psychic gift who uses it. Such a person gives sittings, or readings, to private individuals or to research groups for pay. A professional medium never guarantees any results, nor does he attempt to improve his scoring by fakery or artificial means, such as questions asked of the sitter to supply a clue which can then be fed back to the sitter in different form. Fakery and padding are the true earmarks of the semiprofessional. They exist unfortunately in some spiritualist camps and among some of the readers practicing their trade in one-person churches in the cities of the United States. I refer to these people as semi-professionals because in violating their trust they no longer are entitled to the term *professional*. It is up to the public to sort out the good from the bad. Occasionally a once-powerful medium no longer has the gift, and in order to maintain his standing will pad his readings with common knowledge, guesswork, and material culled from questioning the sitters. But fortunately these people are few.

In this chapter we will not deal with anyone who does not have the highest professional standards. But taking money for one's psychic work is not the only mark of the professional. Another, of course, is a reasonably consistent performance record under varying conditions and with a large number of individuals as sitters. It is entirely possible to be a professional without taking money for one's work, if one's economic position permits. Such people are by no means superior in any way to those who are paid.

Carolyn Chapman, who passed away in the late '70s, was a great medium, often called "the dean of American mediums." She worked primarily with private clients and had a very fine reputation for accuracy.

Virginia Cloud, a Southern writer who has also passed on, had a record of making accurate prophecies for many years, though she was a nonprofessional in the field.

Betty Dye, a great psychic healer currently living in the Atlanta area, has also shown herself to be a fine medium.

John Gaudry, an Australian professional psychic, has for many years been an active and much-admired psychic reader, with many documented predictions come true.

Irene Hughes, perhaps the best-known medium in the Midwest, has years of work as a reputable and highly skilled psychic to her credit, and has been the subject of several books.

The late Jimmy Jacobs of London, a highly successful amateur medium, made his living as an operator of nightclubs and a producer of revues.

Sybil Leek, at one time considered not only the most colorful psychic but also a great deep-trance medium and scholar, was originally a writer working in television in her native England. After she came to American she sought me out, and we worked together on many cases of hauntings and possession, even traveling together here and abroad. Her books on the paranormal were also successful, and she eventually settled in Florida, where she passed on far too soon.

Bill Linn headed up, along with his wife, a small Spiritualist center in New York City some years ago.

The late Ethel Johnson Meyers, one of the truly great deep-trance mediums in the world, also worked in New York City as a reader and ran a Spiritualist development circle at her studio on New York's West Side.

Dr. N., a medical doctor in California, has used his psychic gift in diagnosing patients with excellent results. He is understandably shy about divulging his name and risking criticism from his medical colleagues. Because of his past record of accuracy regarding predictions made and come true, his visions of the future are particularly disturbing.

Julie Parrish, an actress living in California, has had the gift of predicting events since childhood, and her psychic readings have a reputation for accuracy.

The late Betty Ritter was one of the great psychics in the New York area. A Spiritualist and photography medium, she maintained an amazing track record of predictions made and come true (many of them years later than predicted, but accurate nevertheless).

Shawn Robbins, a young woman residing in New York City, is a professional psychic with an excellent track record.

Frederick Stoessel, originally a financial adviser, eventually turned his psychic gift to world predictions as well as to stock market trends, issuing a newsletter and generally providing often accurate pictures of future developments in the political and business worlds.

Jill Taggert, a writer and actress living in California at the time I queried her, has had premonitions and psychic impressions since childhood and has a respectable accuracy record regarding them.

CHAPTER 6

Future Wars: Predictions and Premonitions from the 1970 Survey

The specter of war is ever present. We have gone through two world wars, the Korean War, and the unfortunate war in Vietnam, and somehow survived all those calamities. But many people seem to dread a future global war far more destructive than any we have already experienced. This is, of course, because of the advances in warfare, especially the development of atomic weaponry. There seems to be a universal feeling that the next world war may result in the ultimate destruction of the planet. Any warnings, even small hints, as to what may be in store for us are therefore of great interest. When I spoke to Dr. N. in San Francisco some years ago and then published his predictions about a bombing attack upon the San Francisco area to occur on December 29, 1970, I did so not to scare my readers but to present, as a reporter, what a man of impeccable background and proven accuracy as a psychic had said. As is frequently the case, dates are unreliable when it comes to psychic predictions, but events themselves do frequently occur as foreseen. I therefore questioned Dr. N. once again recently and repeated what he had said to me several years ago about an attack on San Francisco. He reiterated his original prediction, qualifying it by saying only that the year may have been off; but as he has based his prediction on a vision in which he saw the actual attack, he felt that it was indeed something in our future that would transpire. When I questioned him about the date, December 29, 1970, which he had originally given me for this attack, he explained that he had based his date on the models of automobiles he saw in this vision.

I do not wish to evoke fear. I am just as convinced that individuals will escape destruction if that is their fate, and that individual destiny supersedes mass catastrophes even if the latter are ordained by a higher order than we are presently aware of or understand. That this higher order of things is always in operation I am sure. Consequently I look forward to the difficult years ahead not with fear but with a determination to make myself as useful in my world as I can, so that that same higher order may elect to salvage me when the big showdown comes. I can do no more than that, and I recommend that everyone reading these lines does likewise.

The question I put to all the mediums and psychics I interviewed was always identical. I asked them to submit to an interview without giving them prior notice as to what the questions would be, of course. I then read each question individually and asked for their reply. I stressed my desire not to get logical evaluations of world events, but only intuitively felt, psychically inspired answers. It is, of course, impossible to separate entirely a person's logical thinking or opinions from psychic impressions, but to the extent that this is possible I think that I succeeded in getting material from the unconscious part of these gifted people rather than from their ordinary, everyday minds.

Not every person replied in the same way. Some were able to be specific in their answers and to stick with the questions.

Others were more general in their answers to particular questions or brought in extraneous material. Whenever this extraneous material was also of interest or tied in with the question I left it in the record. I did so on the assumption that all psychic impressions given me here were inspired by outside forces, perhaps by the personalities controlling these mediums, and that it was not up to me to eliminate what seemed to be valid information, even if it was not in direct reply to a question I had asked. Thus the reader will have to evaluate for himself the material that I am presenting here; and even though I will draw certain conclusions, these will be only my conclusions and do not necessarily represent a factual image of the world to come. They may come close to what is in store for us all, but I do not guarantee this in any way.

For myself, I am convinced that where there is smoke there is fire. When so many psychically gifted people predict similar events, and when these same people have a proven record of accuracy in prior predictions, whether of personal or of universal nature, I cannot help feeling that to disregard their predictions just because they are unpleasant or unwanted would be foolish. I therefore accept the image presented by the sum total of these predictions as coming close to the world of tomorrow.

Here then are the questions and the responses I received.

Do you foresee any major war involving the United States during the next ten years, and if so, what sort of war, when, where fought and between what countries, and what outcome?

Carolyn Chapman:

"Yes. China."
Who will win it?
"The U.S.A."
How long will it last?
"A couple of years."

Will there be atomic destruction?
"No. They won't use that."

Virginia Cloud:

"I see no declared war involving the United States during the next ten years. Leaders are becoming more aware of the futility of destructive conflict. Another major war would—*or could*—end all life on earth. Differences will be settled more and more by negotiation. Those taking part in these conferences will come to be increasingly less political. Sociologists and economists will replace politicians at conference tables."

Betty Dye:

"War? Yes . . . major . . . within next ten years . . . between U.S., Europe, Asia, red countries . . . Germany (again) . . . Russian (feeling much more confident with affiliation with Reds), Asian, meaning Red China. Outcome: won by the nation serving and loving God. Matthew 24:6—'And ye shall hear of wars, and rumors of war; see that ye be not troubled; for all these things must come to pass, but the end is not yet.' Matthew 24:14—'And this gospel of the kingdom shall be preached in all the world, for a witness unto all nations; and then shall the end come.' "

John Gaudry:

"I see, around 1973, I feel something will be happening there; I don't know what countries, but around 1973 I see something to do with China. I see the number 6 after this. And I see something to do with a man with the initials G.H. G.H.J. I don't know what that is, but it is the answer to this question."

Irene Hughes:

"Russia will *never* be friends or allies with the U.S. She's going to be more and more afraid of Communist China, but eventually China will tell her what to do and she will have to do what Red China tells her.

"She may get into a corner and start running toward us and want friendship, but we will be fools if we accept her as a friend. I actually feel that there will an attack made upon this country. It will come through the back door of this country through Mexico and not from South America. I feel that this will be a token attack. But I feel that it will actually be in Florida, and it will also touch in Texas, and that it will go to Washington, D.C. And I have predicted that they would move the capital out of Washington. However, I feel that no country will ever take over our nation, not psychologically, nor with nuclear weapons. And that, to me, the most tragic of all wars will begin in 1993, in February of that year. It will be an all-out nuclear war, but we will never be completely destroyed."

The one that you see between Red China and the United States, then, you don't think will be a big war?

"It will go into a big war, but the token—only a token attack will be made on this continent."

Where will the rest of it take place?

"It will take place in the Middle East; it will go on to touch on the shores of Australia, to Alaska, to Greenland, and in that area also. And this is something I'm sure that people have not even expected."

And who will win it?

"I feel that Red China will come out the victor more than any other nation. But we will not be completely controlled ever. I'm saying this because you see I cannot see most of the nuclear war going on in this country, but on other shores."

Do you see any attack on any large cities by nuclear weapons?

"Yes, I do."

What part of the world will not be touched by this?

"I feel that Canada will be the safest—really and truly—the safest nation."

What about Europe?

"No, I do not feel that, because I believe that in Germany, that the Nazis will be on the march again; I've said this, that within twenty-five years they will go back to try to win an old debt. They will never forget what happened to them, and they will certainly be our enemies."

Do you feel that they will be exactly like the Nazis or is this a new movement?

"I feel that it will be a new movement with some of the old ideas still there."

You mean a new leader of some sort?

"A new leader, yes, but with some Hitler ideas."

And what do they do?

"I feel that they plan to really rise up and that there will not be the wall between east and west Germany, again—that will go down—and I also feel that they will spread to other areas in Europe and that they will not only be involved in Europe but also in the U.S."

Do you feel that these will be criminal elements the way the Nazis were in World War II or simply a nationalist movement?

"It will be more than a nationalist movement, because they will be going against another nationality, which will be criminal."

What other nationality?

"Strangely enough, it will be against those people who are not German, or who do not have Nazi ideas. They will—you know—they will not go against the black race, but they will go against the white race."

You mean other nationalities than their own?

"Yes; yes."

Is this in the foreseeable future?

"It is within the next twenty years."

And will any part of Europe not be involved in this?

"Switzerland is going to change, and they will no longer be a neutral area. I believe that small countries are going to be involved in this. Northern Canada will be one of the safest places. And the Midwest is going to be one of the safest places where the nuclear bombing is concerned."

Jimmy Jacobs:

"I do not predict any major war, but I do predict a major conflict involving China and Russia, and Russia will survive."

Sybil Leek:

"No impressions about future wars."

Bill Linn:

"I feel that we will have small wars, which will antagonize us, not a major war. I feel that there will be three or four small wars that we will be getting directly involved in. We will be there to supply arms, manpower, to train soldiers in those countries that need help. Within the next ten years I feel that the United States will be on the verge of a major war, and it will be between us and China. I feel that it will be almost to the point of a major conflict; I feel that it will develop and last possibly three or four weeks, and then it will terminate. I don't feel that it will be a long major war. I see this possibly within the next eight or nine years. I feel that Russia certainly will be an ally of ours, but I feel this conflict between us and the Chinese people."

Ethel Johnson Meyers:

"There are major purposes in those small fracases. The Middle East is very important. It is against Israel."
Do you foresee an open and full-fledged war in Israel during the next ten years?
Yes; but the power that is trying to get and gain the pinnacle of power is subversive, and that is not Russia, but China."
Will the United States be involved in open warfare during the next ten years?
"Yes, but it is not in the Middle East directly. We will have to defend certain portions of this, yes; but the inevitable will hap-

pen in this way. The Russians, who are becoming more capitalistic, will level off with the more socialistic state in this country, and this will make a bridge across the oceans and stand as a bulwark before the onslaught of the Red Chinese. It will stave it off until the latter seventies. Now the Red Chinese have set off a red herring in the Middle East, for the purpose of breaking the company that they are seeing as an inevitable truth, this country and Russia holding hands. And the other purpose, as I said, is to eliminate Israel."

Will they succeed?

"Not at this point, no."

Would you specify this more clearly?

"This will not come off, because the two countries that are opposing Israel—or two, one for and one against—standing in opposition. We will not stand in opposition, but we will hold hands. Russia and this country."

So what will the outcome be?

"The outcome will be that it will be staved off."

Dr. N.:

"The United States and China will be at war. Outcome: Vermont intact, Montana, Wyoming, lower Colorado, Eastern Texas, parts of Kentucky, most of Georgia, all intact. California, Oregon, Washington largely lost due to radioactive fallout from water blasts on coast. Most of the country severely destroyed. 86.6 percent population loss.

"China: missiles at Ulan Bator destroyed by Russia. Is it known that missiles are being built there? I don't know. Are they Chinese or Russian?

"Keriya out, Batang [Paan], Chungking destroyed; Nanking intact; Peking, Paoshan, Mengtze, Nanning [Yungning], Amoy, Hainan, Canton, Taiwan—total destruction. 190 million dead.

"Spain, Portugal, Sweden, much of Africa OK."

To which grim prediction Dr. N. adds this explanatory note.
"I hope the picture I paint is all wrong, as it is rather bleak. Many of my predictions have been wrong, but most are not. I predicted the trouble on *Apollo 13* almost exactly to many friends who now think more seriously about ESP. I told them, 'It may just get back if they can get the electricity and oxygen to hold out.' It wasn't until the morning of the launch that I realized what was going to go wrong. If I had telegraphed you, the FBI would be after me, so I decided to let that one go."
[I assured Dr. N. that the FBI had other problems than persecuting scientists engaged in ESP research as we both are.

Dr. N. continued his remarks concerning the predictions of atomic warfare he had first made to me several years ago and which he was now confirming, so much closer to "curtain time," as it were.]
"Of one thing I am certain: the future is not absolute. For example, I have had many episodes where three versions of the same event have occurred to my inner eye. Eventually one of the three occurred. Perhaps some freedom of choice avails so that variable solutions can be foreseen. This probably explains why some people with ESP get some messages terribly mixed up and others straight. Who knows? Perhaps you do or will find out."

"For some time the Chinese have been working toward an atomic bomb that is small enough to smuggle. They have achieved this. New York is a prime target. They already have a bomb in Moscow, and this aids and fortifies their aggressiveness in dealing with the Russians. Eventually it will bring about World War III. Time is running short."

Julie Parrish:

"I don't feel any destructive war within the next ten years. But there will be little ones here and there, leading up to a very big major one at some time after the ten years. And at that time I don't think there will be anything left of us because of the weapons that we now have. I don't believe there won't be anything left of us at all, but I mean we're going to wipe ourselves back to a Stone Age type of existence. I don't feel Red China is a very big threat at this point. Russia will become our ally."

John Reeves:

"The way I see it is that Russia will try to involve us in a war with China. They will make an attempt to do this and they will not be able to, because trade relationships between this country and China will be reestablished within the next sixteen months. Russia will try to involve us, but no—I don't see it."

Betty Ritter:

"I don't see a major war with Russia; I believe Russia's going to stay out. And I also feel that many of the people there are going to turn against communism. And I feel that Russia will be our ally someday."
What about China?
"I'm thinking of China. I'm afraid of China. I feel that Russia will have trouble with China, but then again, I do feel that Russia can protect itself, and I feel that China will be pushed back. But I don't see a major war. But there will be much trouble. I hear something about Cambodia, and that area, because I feel there will be a revolution there. Also, I do feel that there will be a revolution in Russia, because the people want more freedoms. I do also see something about Israel, and I feel that Golda Meir will be replaced by a man, and I feel that it's due to illness."
Is there going to be a war in Israel?
"No, not at all an out-and-out war; I don't feel that."
Is there a peace settlement in the offing?
"I can see a large table, and I do feel that they will come and settle a peace pact."

Will Red China attack the United States?
"No; no; no."

Shawn Robbins:

"We're going to be forced to take a background part with Israel. This is because the oil business out there is going to be cut off to the United States. There's going to be a lot of problems with the Middle East and the United States, even though it is directed toward Israel; we will become involved because it is going to be our major oil that will be shut off. That will happen in exactly three years' time. After the three years—from the time of from three years to five years—we will be confronted with Russia. From 1975 to 1976, in the latter part of the year, Russia and the United States will be bitter enemies over this whole business with Israel and the Arab countries. There definitely will be a war with one of the Arab countries. Egypt will not be at war with Israel, but it will be a small country that will cause a war with Israel. Then Egypt will step in, but it is not Egypt that starts the war; it's a small country. That's all I come up with for that."

Fredric Stoessel:

"I believe that the United States and Red China are going to fight each other. I have instinctively felt that American troops would tangle with Red Chinese troops. I think that the Russian agriculture is going to fail. I have a feeling that at the time when Russia ceases to be a threat to Red China, Red China will heave a bomb at us. And I don't think it's too far off; I'd say within the next two or three years."
Have you any feeling as to the geographical location that will be involved?
"Well, I think we'll be involved in Laos and Thailand, but I have a feeling that a bomb will be thrown at the United States."

In what part of the United States?
"The west coast somewhere. Or perhaps Chicago; I'm not sure."
Is this an atomic bomb you're talking about?
"I'm talking about a nuclear bomb of some sort. The type that we're trying to build the defenses for now."
Will it be very damaging?
"I think it will be horrifying and it will wake everybody up. I think it will do a lot of damage, yes."
What will happen subsequent to that?
"I think the American people will be very thoroughly aroused, and I think it will be a very short war; it will be taken care of."
What will be the outcome of this war?
"The United States will win the war; there's no doubt about it."
What countries will be involved?
"I think the United States, Britain, France, and China; and Russia will fight Red China."
You say Russia will fight Red China?
"Well, I think they will mobilize what forces they can; at least they'll be on our side. I do not think that China and Russia are going to fight each other, though; I don't feel that at all. That is the prevailing theory right now."

Jill Taggart:

"Yes, a major war within two or three years. It will be a civil war fought on our own streets, brother against brother. This is going to be a bloody decade. They will win who seemingly have less to lose, but these winners—young though they may be—know, in part, the value of winning tomorrow away from yesterday. It's already started, and nothing can stop it now."

Probably the most disturbing prediction concerning future wars was made by Dr. N. of San Francisco and published by me several years ago. I have already mentioned that I checked on his prediction with him recently and was told that the prediction concerning the attack on San Francisco stands, but the date might be off. Apparently many readers were equally impressed with Dr. N.'s precise and painstakingly clear predictions. On January 27, 1970, I received a letter from Yukon, Canada, in which a reader referred to the doctor's predictions. Without having read my book at the time, Brian Lloyd had an almost identical dream while staying in northern Alberta, Canada. His dream occurred on December 27, 1967. Mr. Lloyd was then staying at an oil field and camp called Zama Lake. The very first night he stayed there he had almost the same dream as Dr. N., involving vapor trails and a mushroom cloud. He clearly saw that he found himself in the San Francisco Bay area of the west coast of the United States. He knew only that it was a large city, but he did not know which one. The next morning, upon awakening, he felt very disturbed by his dream. "I can still recall the last of that dream after seeing the mushroom cloud. I remember falling to my knees, hands clasped as if in prayer, and after that I guess I awoke." Mr. Lloyd is a laborer, married to a schoolteacher. His interest in psychic literature is recent. He emphasized that his dream had occurred to him before my book saw print.

But Mr. Lloyd is not the only person whose visionary dreams—or dream visions, if you prefer—closely parallel Dr. N.'s predictions. Swedish-born Mrs. Ingrid Olofsson of San Francisco has had psychic experiences for some time, ever since she was a teenager in her native country. One particularly vivid dream vision stands out in her recollections. This happened in 1963, and although she was married at the time, she and her husband had as yet no children. In the dream she saw herself and her husband looking down a road with trees on one side. Suddenly she saw several flying saucers coming from the right, and when she pointed them out to her husband, he grabbed one of them, which seemed about two feet in diameter and aluminum-colored. In the dream she made him let this flying saucer go, and he threw it up into the air. A second later, it came back and a voice from inside the saucer said to her, "You have earned a free trip to Heaven," and away it went. After this somewhat unusual experience the dream turned from black and white to full color. She had the distinct impression that there was someone she must look for. As she walked around looking for this person, there was a hum in the air like a swarm of bees. It was a beautiful sunset now and the sky was pink. She and her husband looked up into the sky and saw a fantastic number of Chinese planes covering the sky from horizon to horizon. The setting sun was still barely lighting up the planes in the air and she could see the red wing lights like fireflies in the sky. Then bombs started falling all around them and exploding, making craters in the ground. They started to run, and she found the person she was seeking and it was her daughter. She grabbed her by the arm and ran as fast as she could. The girl was then about six or seven years of age, as she noticed in her dream, which ended at this point. This dream occurred before Mrs. Olofsson had a daughter. It was only on August 26, 1964, that she gave birth to a little girl.

Mrs. Elsie Maye Oakley, of San Francisco, California, has a B.A. in Education and is a professional teacher. She is married and has two children. Her husband, also a teacher, is a retired colonel in the United States Army. Mrs. Oakley has had a number of psychic experiences and dream visions over the years. In July of 1968 she reported to me a vision in which she very clearly saw a map of the world with the continents plainly in view. Suddenly, upon each of the continents in turn beginning with Europe and then on to Africa, Asia, North and South America, and Australia, there appeared to her, somewhat like a smoke signal, a giant mushroom cloud such as is produced by an atomic explosion. She did not feel the order of appearance by continents significant; rather she felt at the time that it meant that the world would be subjected to a total atomic attack.

Mrs. Barbara Z., a psychology graduate of the University of Illinois, has taught physical education and worked as a social worker in and around Chicago, Illinois, and is the mother of two boys. Over the years she has had many psychic experiences and déjà vu feelings. Since her husband is a medical doctor, she treats these matters perhaps more seriously and cautiously than an ordinary housewife might. Nevertheless, these psychic feelings keep recurring to her, and she has observed them carefully and closely. On August 5, 1969, she communicated with me. She recalled that, when a teenager, she had a strong premonition that sometime after she was married and had children, there would be a surprise atomic attack on Chicago, and if she wasn't careful, she would be part of it. She felt, at that time, that it would happen in the fall on a sunny day, but she did not get any impression as to which year. She has also had feelings about atomic warfare at other places than Chicago, and what would happen if she herself were at those places and where she would find safety.

In the spring of 1968 I was contacted by Mrs. Elaine Atkinson, of northern California. She had seen me on a San Francisco television program and wished to discuss with me a very disturbing psychic vision concerning San Francisco. I managed to speak to her on Thanksgiving of 1968 and to confirm some of the statements she had made in a letter to me earlier that year.

"Several years ago," she stated, "actually, in 1963, I was expecting my son, who will be five years old on October 1, 1968. I was then taking a course in civil defense. Parts of my vision upset me more than I thought, especially seeing pictures of poor, defenseless children wandering in the streets, so to speak half-dead, and of course no one around to take care of them. I thought of these scenes so much at the time and remember lying in bed thinking of all this, when something told me not to worry because my child would be at least seven years old before anything like this would happen. This bothers me now, as Dr. N.'s prediction of the date would make my youngest child just seven years old at the time." Of course, I calmed Mrs. Atkinson as best I could, explaining that dates are rarely if ever correct when it comes to psychic predictions. Nevertheless, she had felt also that San Francisco would be subjected to an atomic attack sometime in the future.

What does it all mean? Professional mediums and amateurs alike seem to have tuned in on some war involving the continental United States in the not-so-distant future. Fifteen professional mediums and five amateur mediums have been consulted for an answer to the question about war involving the United States. Out of these twenty-one voices, only five of these see no major war involving the United States in the future. The others see a war of varying duration and intensity, but in all cases the outcome is favorable to our side. I have often felt that even the most precise predictions of catastrophes may also be interpreted merely as warnings that such events may take place unless the course of human events is altered. Whether or not these visions of war are warnings at the eleventh hour to sway humanity from its destructive path, or whether these are predictions of inflexible, unalterable events already set in motion is something only the future will tell.

CHAPTER 7

Tomorrow's Leaders

Since men make politics, and the politics of nations determine the future of those nations, it is always of interest to try to fathom the personalities of tomorrow's leaders, and the trends by which certain nations will be thrust into the limelight while others will fade from it. I decided to ask the question about tomorrow's leaders of all those psychics participating in my program, to see what material could be obtained concerning the leaders, and then try to evaluate the trends one might conceivably expect from such leaders.

Who will be the leaders of the world ten years hence? What will they represent, and how will they come into power?

Carolyn Chapman:

"Wow! What a question. I think every state in the union should be a sovereign state."
[I repeated the question and asked who she thought would be president of the United States ten years from now.]
"I feel it may be someone from Europe; a European who was born on European soil but who has lived here all his life."

[I pointed out that to allow a foreign-born person to become president, we would have to change the Constitution.]
"We would have to, and I think the Constitution is going to be changed."
What about Russia?
"I don't feel Russia is our enemy. There will be valuable changes there, too."
Do you feel anything concerning the new leaders in Russia?
"I think they are people who are on their way up now, but there is not anyone who is leading now who will be the leader in the next few years."
Do you foresee any change in the Communist system in Eastern Europe?
"Yes, I do. It will be going down. These countries will have to get on their own feet again."
Do you foresee any war between Russia and the United States?
"No, I don't. I think Russia is our friend, and I think they are going to be with us."
And what about Czechoslovakia?
"They will restore their freedom, definitely."

Virginia Cloud:

"The United States will lead the world in ten years, as will China. Russia will be a weak third, or maybe even fourth. Once China has rid herself of her radical leaders and is accepted by the U.N., she will move forward. The mind of the Chinese is too philosophical to embrace permanently many of the doctrines of the past decade. Age, wisdom is still respected among the thinkers of China. China, I feel, will in time be our friend again. Richard Nixon will prove to be one of our finest presidents, growing in respect even by his former detractors. His health will suffer from the burden of his job and from the seriousness with which he regards his responsibilities, and there will be narrow escapes from assassination attempts, even perhaps a slight injury, but he will recover and emerge more respected and admired than when he took office."

Betty Dye:

"I am dim on the actual leaders. There definitely is a young eccentric, radical, sadistic person approaching in ten years from Russia. This young man will cause great toil and turmoil. He is directly involved, partly the cause of the coming great war. He will not be like any previous tyrant coming out of Russia; he will be unique unto himself."

John Gaudry:

"I get a big letter *O*. I don't know if it's an initial, or represents a zero or a target, but when you asked me this question, this big *O* came up on my inner screen."

Jimmy Jacobs:

"In ten years' time the leader—the American president—will be someone who is completely unknown today and not at this moment in politics. Somebody who comes from a farming background. And I predict that in that time the first Jewish president will be elected. In Russia there will be the first liberal Communist leader. He will be elected in precisely ten years from now. Although many of the hardcore Communists will be dispensed with, there will not be a repetition of the Stalin era, and none of these people will be imprisoned. In England, a back-bencher—that is, a person who is in the House of Commons now but is currently of no special importance—will suddenly gain prominence, and the first Liberal prime minister will be elected with the help of the Conservative party, which will by then have waned in popularity."

Bill Linn:

"In ten years hence, I feel that China will be a major power, the United States will be a major power, and Russia will be also. I feel that within ten years these three major powers will still dominate in the world's affairs. I do feel that the smaller countries will combine their resources in men, money, and intelligence, and will eventually challenge the three majors. I feel that the United States will still have a democracy within the next ten years, but eventually, after this period, the democracy as we know it today will change. In China you are going to have more revolutionaries, causing revolutions within the country. We will be challenged from the Orientals in a very strong way, as they develop their mechanical and technological means. Russia will be a kind of ally with us in the next major war. I feel that we will have this war against China, and that it will be a short one, not a long, drawn-out deal. It's going to end as quickly as the Egyptian-Israeli War, except that instead of seven days it will take three to four weeks. And then the great leaders will come to their consciousness, will come to that awareness and will realize that the continuation of war will be total destruction, total annihilation, and they will shut it off very quickly."

Ethel Johnson Meyers:

"The leaders of tomorrow will assert their power, and that is the reason why this country will have a great need for holding back the one great onslaught of the Red Chinese. They are too crowded; they are in necessity of land that is tillable and they do want power and recognition again. They were once the top nation."

Will they attack America with atom bombs?

"Around the later '70s and early '80s, yes."

Will they succeed in destroying major cities?

"No. There are devices that can detect many things. They will do damage, yes."

Will there be an atomic war between the United States and Russia?
"No."
Will there be a civil war in the United States between black and white people?
"There is already."
Will it be much different and worse?
"It will be violent, and it will be passive. It will end when there is understanding of the religious feelings, and when these feelings come under the control of individuals."
Will there still be communism in Russia?
"Not as we know it now."
Will there be freedom for people behind the Iron Curtain, such as in Czechoslovakia?
"It is all softening, going toward a more pliable state, because they are in need of the people. Within the latter part of the next ten years, the Iron Curtain will disappear."
Will we be able to travel freely back and forth, both from Russia to the West, and from the West to Russia?
"During the truce, there will be such travel, yes."
When does the truce start?
"It is on the threshold now; it looks to me like '71."
What about China during the period of truce? Will she attack either Russia or the United States?
"There will be sporadic but not very serious conflicts."
Will Mao Tse-tung die soon?
"Yes, within three years. The successors will be of the same kind, even stronger."
Will Israel be in the same condition it is now, ten years hence?
"It will have gained, but always with strife."
Will there be open, full-fledged warfare between Israel and the Arabs in the next ten years?
"Always. But not openly. They cannot, without the support of this country and Russia. Russia is going to make a right about-face, because it needs this country to stave off China."

When will this happen?

"I believe in '71 these things begin. And Russia will not allow the Arabs to crush Israel."

[The answers received here from Ethel Johnson Meyers's control, Albert, seem to fit more properly into the chapter dealing with future wars, but as they were received in answer to my question concerning the leaders and the leading nations of tomorrow, I feel that they belong here. If Albert feels that the countries named herein—the United States, Russia, China, and Israel—are among the leaders of tomorrow, then he is, of course, right in so replying. The next psychic person similarly refers to Israel as one of the leading nations of tomorrow, so perhaps this is not simply an error in replying to a question, but a deliberate attempt to point out who the future leaders among nations will be in years to come.]

Dr. N.:

"Ten years from now, Spain, Africa, Israel will be in far greater power."

John Reeves:

"In spite of world conditions now, I feel that Russia and the United States will continue to be the leading countries of the world. Red China becomes more of a major power because we will be recognizing her. I also feel that Nixon will be elected for another term."

Shawn Robbins:

"All I can see is the figure 8 and a very young leader. I also get the word *sister* or *brother*. Russia is going to have a lot of problems in their leadership. There will be dissension among the people, especially the young people. But the younger people will not get control. In ten years' time Russia will be friendly with the United States, because of the new leader. This new leader is a young person, aged forty-three, and he will be someone's sister or brother, someone who is very

important. There seems to be an aristocratic type of family that
has power there."
Do you get any initials for that person?
"Yes, I keep seeing rubies, so that could mean the letter *R*; and
something white."
*But how does this gel with your thinking that there will be a war
between Russia and the United States?*
"No, there won't be a war. Russia and the United States will be
more friendly. And there will be trouble in Yugoslavia, an uprising. It involves a secret underground group. It is present in all
the Communist countries, but Yugoslavia will be the first to
have an uprising. But it won't be like in Czechoslovakia, where
Russia came in. This is definitely something else that happens,
that they are revolting against. Not like the Hungarian Revolution either."
Is it going to be successful?
"Yes. Yugoslavia will be coming into the news soon. About six
months from now Yugoslavia is going to be one of the first
countries that won't be so tightened by the Communist rule."
*What about China and her relationship with the United States and
Russia?*
"Nineteen seventy-seven is a very bad time for the United States
and China. I feel a conflict then. It's not the United States that
will be bombed. New York City does not have to worry. But
China will be bombed; a quarter of the country will be
bombed. The United States will not be fighting alone. Russia
will be involved also, against China. It will be a war like the
Vietnam War, except more sophisticated. Missiles will be used.
The United States and Russia will be on the same side, although
they are not fighting together. Although they are not trying to,
each one will help the other."
Will there be any atomic weapons?
"A lot of missiles will be used."
What will the outcome be?
"We'll still be fighting in 1977. It will end in 1981."

And what will the result be?

"This is when changes in our government will take place. Russia and the United States will be very close in 1981. Russia will have a new form of government then, similar to that in the United States. China will continue to be a Communist country after 1981. They are defeated, but one cannot trust them. Because in 1990 China becomes a world power. That is when the first major war occurs. China will be rebuilding herself, and whatever happened before then were just little things. The real next world war is not 1980, but 1990."

Fredric Stoessel:

"I think your world leaders will to a great degree be coming out of the Middle East. I think the religious leaders are going to come out of Soviet Russia, but I think that's more than ten years. Nevertheless, I look to Soviet Russia for religious leaders. The Middle East, I think, is going to produce the great political leaders of our time."

In what way?

"Well, in the sense that government and economy ties in with the West, but the African people are not going to develop leaders to influence the West. I feel that someone is going to come out of the Middle East."

Do you have any feelings for specific personalities?

"I have a feeling that Nasser could be a very helpful man. I see him as a good influence in the long run."

How do you see the outcome of the Arab-Israeli conflict?

"I have mixed feelings. I see commotion there for a long time. I have no solution; just turmoil; maybe ten, twenty years."

It is interesting to note here, also, that Jeane Dixon predicted years ago that a great world leader would be born in Egypt who would eventually emerge and become the single most powerful leader in the world. Similarly, Nostradamus predicted that a man of Near Eastern background would become the scourge of mankind in a war leading up to Armageddon.

Jill Taggart:

"The leaders will be our youngsters, and they will represent personal freedom and privacy. They will strive for a 'one world' government, but they will come into power through violence."

All the psychics queried seemed to consider Russia, not surprisingly, a future ally. This, of course, is not necessarily psychic forecasting, but good common sense. There are many people in this country who do not have an ounce of ESP who feel the same way. But the 1970s did not indicate any such rapprochement. Russia was still adamant in her attitudes toward the United States, and America hadn't given an inch. Therefore, what may have been hopeful thoughts and wishful thinking to the nonpsychic were perhaps real psychic insights to those gifted with ESP; it is conceivable that these individuals foresaw actual events. Only one or two of the mediums queried does not see a major attack by China upon this country. But then again, the question of what is a major war and a minor war is also debatable. In this respect, all mediums questioned by me agreed: there will be conflict with China.

Perhaps ten years is too short a time to see major changes taking place in the spiritual attitudes of people. I am somewhat disappointed to see that there is not in store for us a major uplifting, a major overhauling of our spiritual attitudes toward life itself and our mission on earth. It seems to me that we will simply be continuing on the same perilous road we are on now, if the psychics are seeing things right. This tends to reinforce a widely held belief among religious people that God must first destroy the wicked before the good can rise and take their rightful places in the scheme of things. But there is perhaps some comfort to be found

in the thought that many of us will be around to observe
how accurate have been the predictions made by my psychic friends.

Clearly, the psychics queried by me in 1970 had for the
most part very clouded crystal balls! As of today, few of the
prophecies made by this group have come to pass. But, as we
have previously seen, time is an elusive element in the world
of prophecy. Are these prophets wrong on their dates but perhaps right regarding events yet to come? Today, in 1995, it does
not look likely. But the future has a way of presenting sudden
changes and surprises.

CHAPTER 8

The Question of
Natural Catastrophes

Probably the most publicized predictions in recent years concerned the state of California—whether it would sink into the sea or continue to flourish. Psychics from many parts of the country have predicted its imminent demise, and as early as 1969 people actually thought of leaving their houses in California in order not to be caught by the impending disaster. Much of this frenzy can be traced directly to the writings of the late Edgar Cayce, who has been very precise in predicting certain changes in the earth. Among these changes are catastrophes befalling both the west coast and the Atlantic seaboard. But Cayce is somewhat more vague when it comes to dates. None of his predictions pinpointed a date, although they were very specific in details.

Now, we must make a distinction between prophecies and ordinary predictions based upon educated guesses, technical knowledge, and some form of intuition, which is quite common with a large number of people. For example, it doesn't take a psychic to predict that the San Andreas Fault in California will, at some future date, be the site of large-scale earthquakes and destruction. It is also very likely that volcanic activity will in the future increase in the Hawaiian Islands. Geological teams have for years kept an eye on the development of these natural disturbances, and they are practically unanimous in warning that a catastrophe is a distinct possibility within a matter of years. Despite a devastating earthquake in San Francisco in 1989, very few people in California have actually pulled up stakes and gone elsewhere. Even fewer are worried about a natural catastrophe occurring in New York City, even though there exists underneath Manhattan a deep fracture, discovered accidentally when Consolidated Edison wanted to dig even deeper into Manhattan's bedrock. There is an element of acceptance among all of us, perhaps mixed with a basic disbelief that such horrible things could actually befall us. Life goes on despite the danger signals, and predictions by psychics are not likely to change this attitude among average people.

Do you foresee any geographical changes in the not-too-distant future through natural catastrophes such as earth- or seaquakes, tidal waves, and changes in earth temperature, and if so, when, where, and how?

Carolyn Chapman:

"There is going to be devastation within the next few years. I see a very great flood of some kind. And as for California, I see this clairvoyantly, and I see it dividing—that is, two great strips of land, one going one way and one the other way. There will be landslides having to do with California, not too far from Santa Barbara. In addition, I see an earthquake in the area around San Francisco, on the border of San Francisco. There is going to be a lot of devastation in the West, and there will be some of it in Europe, too. Something about the Dutch West Indies—I am not sure, it could be Aruba, but it is definitely Dutch. I also get the feeling about devastation around a wharf, where there are boats tied up. This is in the West."

Virginia Cloud:

"Industry and man himself will bring about many geographical changes in the next ten years. I see floods, tidal waves, earthquakes, forest fires of tragic and widespread destruction. Temperature changes will be noticeable by colder winters and hotter summers, especially in the western hemisphere and more so in the United States."

Betty Dye:

"Yes, earthquakes and floods in diverse places, especially coastal regions. The summers will grow shorter, the winters longer and more severe all over."

John Gaudry:

"I see things happening in Hawaii, and something around Vancouver. I feel that within five years the west coast—something around Santa Rosa, I believe—will have some very big things happening. I see the figure 3 to 5, so I would say it is three to five years from now. I feel something going away, falling."

On October 20, 1969, John Gaudry reported a dream to me. In this dream he saw himself in a railroad-type flat, and his mother was with him. He heard her say, "There will be a terrific earthquake coming soon," and in the same breath, "It will probably snow tonight." John Gaudry assumed that this concerned New York City.

On December 3, 1969, John Gaudry communicated to me another significant dream:

> Another prediction for the record which I sincerely hope will not happen. In a dream state three days ago I seemed to be in a ship which was wrecked in mountainous waves off the coast of Hawaii. Of course, these waves had been reported December 2. But as I didn't record this in any way, it can be disregarded, except maybe for the fact that in my last letter to you, which

was filled with material regarding earthquakes, I did mention that when the first snow fell in New York, we could expect another quake. This seems to time it. In the dream I am here reporting, I remember that after the ship had left Hawaii, I found myself in some tremendous seaquake. This time I was told we were in the Hudson Bay area, up in northern Canada. Judging from past experiences of my dream "catastrophes," they seem to happen within four to five days of the actual dream. The scene was very vivid, with enormous waves and piles of gigantic logs crashing all over the place. There also seemed to be a lot of people, especially children, tossing around in the water.

Timing is always a difficult element in predictions. So far as I know this dire prediction concerning a seaquake and tidal wave has not yet come to pass in the area indicated by Mr. Gaudry.

Irene Hughes:

"Two years ago I predicted earthquakes in California, Alaska, and Hawaii, and some of these have already happened. This, I thought, was only the beginning. There will be a volcano in the Hawaiian Islands that will erupt, and some land will fall off into the sea. I feel that all these natural catastrophes will destroy more than nuclear weapons will. I don't think there will be the destruction of a major city involved, but there will be tragedies in major cities through fire, riots, but not by nature. There is also the possibility that another major earthquake will hit Alaska, around Anchorage."

Jimmy Jacobs:

"A natural catastrophe—a seaquake—will strike at the Philippines and there will be approximately 300,000 casualties. This will be the worst natural disaster of all time. There will be violent earthquakes within a hundred-mile radius of Tokyo, with casualties of 80,000. I predict that in Australia there will be a change of earth temperature caused by some sort of volcano. This will produce no casualties but will be of great geological interest."

Sybil Leek:

"My biggest impression is of a new continent with temples and man-made structures which will appear. It will link up with the Maya temples of Mexico. There is a line drawn to Bimini and Cat Island. Everything found there will have a counterpart in the Yucatán; measurements will be the same. But treasure-seekers will find nothing of importance. The importance will be the city itself and its structure."

Bill Linn:

"There will be many geographical changes. The seasons are going to shift. You're going to have bodies of land coming out of the ocean that have never previously been seen or explored. I feel that a major area will appear in the Atlantic Ocean. There will be a small section of land. I also feel that around Hawaii there will be sightings of land, and that the ocean and the waters will lose their shallowness, and divers will see changes appear. Our whole world is going through many seasonal changes. Here in New York I feel that our seasons are going to change also, and instead of having four basic seasons there will be just two. It will be extremely cold and extremely warm. Man himself will cause the destruction of land, through his exploration of atomic and hydrogen power. I feel that current offshore drilling for oil in California is dangerous. Man-made explosions may be causing trouble. I also see that within the next ten years there will be areas which will make us think to realize that there were other civilizations which have preceded us. There will be found different objects that will be evidence for this."

Ethel Johnson Meyers:

"There will be changes, but the major ones will be the perpendicular standings of the poles. I foresee no major changes involving major cities, at least not in this generation. There will be small catastrophes, yes, but no sudden sinkings, including California and New York."

Dr. N.:

"I foresee a temperature rise in the next ten years of approximately eight degrees. There will be a sharp rise in three years."

Julie Parrish:

"I feel something very strange about California. I feel that in the very near future it is going to go—not all of it, to be sure; the Los Angeles and Santa Barbara area. I know there are going to be changes in the poles, and places will become tropical that were not before, and vice versa. But I really don't have any feeling as to when."

John Reeves:

"There will be something in the area between California and Baja California, as if there is a separation between those two. I do not see the California coast melting into the sea as many people have said, but I do see some sort of a separation in which Baja becomes an island. I also see tidal waves around the area of the Caribbean and off the South Atlantic. It seems to me there will be five or six new islands arising in that area within the next ten years. I do not get any destruction of major cities in this country within the next ten years."

Betty Ritter:

"I see a very bad flood in Italy, in a place starting with the letters *P-o*. And there will be some landslides in California. There seems to be a very large earthquake coming from Canada, swinging out west—perhaps Michigan and then farther west. I also feel an eruption of Mount Vesuvius, in Italy, and people should be very careful in that area."

On January 5, 1970, Betty Ritter felt impelled to warn me of an earthquake in California the same year, at the same time adding that I would not be anywhere close to it. But she felt this to be an earthquake or a landslide, and although she did not insist on 1970 as the date for it, she felt it was fairly close.

Shawn Robbins:

"This is something I definitely feel. Everybody thinks the earth is going to disappear, and especially New York City and California. But that's not how it's going to happen. It doesn't happen overnight; it will take many years. I'll describe it as I go along. First thing that happens is that we're going to have weather changes, starting with the rains. We won't think anything of it. We'll have heavy rains, especially in California. But within the next three years, little by little, things will get pretty bad in California. There will be weather storms of this type also, and I feel that from the rains and all that things will start. The ground will loosen up a lot, and people will be moving out; houses will be unsafe—they'll start sinking toward the ocean. The ocean will move a little closer inland. The tides will not go back where they were before. It may only be two feet, but that's how it's going to start. Gradually the tides will creep up on California's shores. There'll be hurricanes too, but that will be mainly in the Caribbean area. In Florida also the water is going to creep inland toward the shore—maybe two feet at a time. This will start in 1972. By 1974 you will start to feel it here in New York City. California won't have it in the San Francisco area, but there we will have a small tremor in the earth. It will be a very important tremor; it is not in San Francisco itself, but toward the mountain regions. This will cause some openings in the ground, but no damage, because it is not in a residential section. But we will start to worry, and then something really big will happen. This will be in California—not in San Francisco, but inland from there. The direction is out of San Francisco. It is the area just before the Rockies, if you are going in that direction. They will have a problem in that area. I hope there are no people there, because this area is going to be flooded and will be under water. If there are dams there, they may burst, and the water remains. Whatever happens, the water is not going to get out to sea again. A landslide will occur in Turkey and Iran, killing over 100 people—this will be in 1970 to 1971. Also in 1970 expect lava to flow from a volcano and leave people homeless. This is a volcano that has only recently been active again. In 1970 also a country which begins with *I*—perhaps Indonesia—will have many problems because of natural earth disasters that will strike the country, such as earthquakes and landslides."

In October 1969 Shawn Robbins put down in writing certain other predictions. She felt that New York City would feel an earth tremor within six and a half to eight years. It would be somewhere 300 miles outside of New York City, but would not cause any damage to the city. "A natural disaster involving flooding will happen four years from now in the area around New Hampshire."

Fredric Stoessel:

"I think there are going to be many earthquakes, and we are going to see natural disasters such as we have had in Turkey. I think they are going to occur in Roman Catholic countries, and countries that have been heavily tied to an institutional type of religion. I have a feeling in the United States we are going to see more fires and sinking of land. As for California, I see fires; more than anything else, I have a feeling fires are the problem there."

Jill Taggart:

"I and two psychic friends feel there will be an earthquake in California, probably during the month of October. We sense the presence of water; also, that the Los Angeles basin will be largely destroyed, that the San Fernando Valley will suffer damage but will survive better than the city, and that the Sunset Strip will be destroyed totally. My friends have seen the creation of at least one new hill. We feel heat will be connected with the quake."

Of the sixteen people questioned about natural catastrophes, only four came up with hopeful predictions. Twelve were quite firm in their view that earthquakes, tidal waves, and other natural catastrophes would indeed befall our country. The majority felt that California was the focal point of these disasters, although New York was often mentioned as well. Even assuming that every one of the mediums queried has read Edgar Cayce's predictions, there is sufficient variety and individuality in the wording of the predictions here published to discount for the most part any influence by the famous "sleeping prophet."

But to say that people predict catastrophes because there is talk in the air of such catastrophes is really begging the issue. Quite obviously, where there is talk about some very specific event, it cannot be entirely due to either fear, wishful thinking in cases of pleasant things, or simply a general attitude toward the kind of phenomena one predicts. There must be some basis of fact. I don't think that the San Andreas Fault itself is sufficiently well known to cause the large number of predictions made by nonprofessional mediums *all over the world* concerning a natural disaster in California. These reports have come to me persistently over a number of years, and I have selected a few at random to illustrate that people who have no interest in the occult, people who are not professionals in any sense, nevertheless do apparently get premonitory dreams, warnings of impending disasters—all of them linking up with the predictions made by professional mediums concerning catastrophes in the United States, especially California.

A case in point is Mrs. Elsie May Oakley of California. Mrs. Oakley is a teacher and housewife, and she is married to a teacher. She has had ESP experiences and premonitory visions for a number of years. In particular, she reports a vision that occurred to her on the night of July 12, 1968. In this she saw the Yosemite Valley, in Yosemite National Park in California, a place she knows well. The valley floor is at an elevation of 4,000 feet; the great granite cliffs tower over it another 3,000 feet. She saw one of the great monoliths, called El Capitan, with Half Dome and Clouds' Rest—two other huge granite formations—rising to 8,000- and 9,000-foot elevations at the eastern end of the valley. Suddenly there was a huge wave of water curling over El Capitan; then more waves rolled in and splashed all around the rim of the cliffs, watering the valley, and finally even curled up from behind and over Clouds' Rest, the highest point immediately surrounding the Yosemite Valley. Her impression was of an enormous tidal wave, inundating the whole of Yosemite. She realized, of course, in view of the great elevation, that this would be a fearsome tidal wave indeed if it could reach such a place, since Yosemite Valley is some 85 to 100 miles east of the Pacific Ocean, as well as so high above sea level.

The next day she reread *The Sleeping Prophet*, in which Cayce's predictions about a California earthquake of disastrous proportions are told. She realized then that there might be some connection between her vision and the material in Jesse Stearn's book. At that point she contacted me, sending a copy of her letter to the Association for Research and Enlightenment in Virginia Beach, Virginia. Mrs. Oakley is a serious person, a trained observer in every sense of the word. One can hardly dismiss her kind of precognitive vision, even though the newspapers, at the time when it was fashionable to predict disasters for California, tried to make light of all such premonitions. "They've got California going down the drain," said *The New York Daily News*. "In recent weeks predictions of doom have increased, talk of calamity comes up on radio and TV shows along with references to strange astrological charts. The day most mentioned: April 14." An earthquake did occur in April 1969.

Bonnie Jean H. is a housewife who has worked at various jobs, as a salesclerk, a cook, and others. A native of Los Angeles, she was thirty-two years old at the time when she first contacted me. She, her husband, and four children live in the Sierras, the mountains they love so much. Mrs. H. is active in her church, does not drink, and leads a pretty average small-town life. The first time she was aware of the fact that there was something in her make-up different from that of most other people around her was at the time in 1954 when the family lived at an old stagecoach station turned into dwelling quarters, in Strawberry Valley. Apparently the old stagecoach station was haunted; Mrs. H. felt watched, although no one could be seen. In houses she lived in subsequently there were strange noises, appearances she could not account for—such as swinging doors when there was no one about—and other psychic phenomena generally associated with hauntings. She took all this in stride, since she had seen her own mother demonstrate ESP talents some years before. But Mrs. H.'s experiences with haunted houses are not the subject of this book. Her premonitions became more pronounced as time went on. In 1955 she and her husband were in a car en route to Healdsburg, California. Suddenly she felt compelled to stop the car and explain that she wanted to go home, for if they continued they would all be in a wreck. There were two other people with them, and since the majority insisted on their continuing, they did so. Sure enough, after her husband took over the wheel, they were in a wreck and it was a close call for everyone. There were other instances of warnings that occurred to her. In one case she was able to prevent a boiler from blowing up in the apartment next door to hers. She took these incidents of prophecy as natural parts of herself until the event that caused her to contact me disturbed her more than anything else she had ever experienced in the area of extrasensory perception.

In the second week of October 1968, a friend visited Mrs. H. from Quincy, California. She casually remarked that there had been an earthquake at Anchorage, Alaska. This amazed Mrs. H., and she heard herself say, "Anchorage? I thought Los Angeles was next." Shortly thereafter, she found herself in bed early in the morning. Her husband had left for work and it was still too early to get up so she tried to get back to sleep. It was about seven o'clock, and she was somewhere in the state between sleep and wakefulness, trying to keep her mind a blank so that she could get back to sleep for a few more precious minutes. As she was drifting off, she was half asleep and yet she seemed to hear the news on the television set or radio, and she heard the announcer talking about the war in Vietnam, the bombing, casualties, deaths, fighting, and so forth. Then she heard him put the papers down and rustle them, and he then started to talk about there being no news about the disastrous earthquake that had destroyed the central valley of California. He said that rescuers hadn't gotten into the area yet to assess the damage and that the center of the quake seemed to be located in the Sacramento-Stockton area. Appalled, Mrs. H. jumped out of bed and charged out of her bedroom. The TV set was off; there wasn't any radio playing, either. She bawled the kids out for turning the news off when there was such important news on the TV. Her children looked at her in amazement; no one had touched either radio or TV. Yet she had clearly heard the announcer describe a disastrous earthquake in the Sacramento-Stockton area. When Mrs. H. realized the implications of her experience, she became frightened. Not only was she upset by her psychic experience, but also she was puzzled as to why she had been given advance notice of an earthquake in the central valley of California when she herself had always thought that Los Angeles would be affected.

Quite obviously Mrs. Oakley's Yosemite Valley vision and Mrs. H.'s premonition of disaster in the central valley of California have something in common. They point at inland areas of California as the probable place where catastrophes may strike. This is entirely different from the overall tenor of most predictions made during the last few years. Every one of the "prophets of doom" has singled out the coastline, and Los Angeles and San Francisco in particular, as the areas most likely to be affected. But Mrs. Oakley and Mrs. H. are by no means alone in their tuning in to future disasters in California.

Mrs. Mary Shewell, another California resident, has always had psychic experiences. The one she found particularly impressive, if not upsetting, was a dream vision that occurred to her in April of 1968. She dreamed of a terrible earthquake. "When it was over, there were just broken cracks in the earth. No one was left but me, and way up on a mountain I could see my deceased Dad with outstretched hands waiting for me."

May Siracusano, also a California resident, has had psychic experiences all her life. She has seen ghosts in houses she lived in, and she has had instances of telepathic communications. But, again, one particular incident disturbed her far more than any of her other numerous ESP experiences. Two years before she contacted me—that is, in March of 1968—she had a vivid vision. She saw an underground force, almost like a living thing, blow up like a geyser. People were running, screaming; someone seemed to fall into a big hole in the ground, while others did not. Then she saw a beautiful scroll with names written on it, and she felt that these were the names of people who would be saved. Then, a couple of months before she contacted me in 1970, she heard the words "This is the last year California will be as it is now." May Siracusano connects the two experiences and feels that they forebode disaster for some portion of California at some point in the future.

Another vision occurred to Mrs. Herbert Mallett, a Los Angeles resident. In late September of 1967 she had a vivid dream in which she found herself in a room with some people and someone seemed to be assigning each one of them a task. As she was waiting for her assignment, her name was called. She was then asked what she had done for the world and at this point the dream ended. It seemed to her that she was being called to account in some way. The same night she went back to sleep and in another dream she saw many people, houses, lumber, cars, and her own family being washed over a large embankment into the water. It seemed to her that all of Los Angeles was floating away. She herself was lying on a plank just wide enough for her body, and she was moving toward the embankment in the water. As she was just about to slide into the water itself, a figure in a white robe and skull cap came out of the sky and reached out for her.

Juanita Gregg lives in Sacramento, California. She has had many psychic experiences of the less than spectacular kind. She would know a letter was in her mailbox before it arrived and who it was from, or she would foretell accidents that later happened just as she had foreseen them. On one occasion, she foretold the return of a navy man related to her, at a time when he was absolutely not expected back. Nevertheless, the young man arrived just as she had predicted.

She contacted me on June 30, 1969. "Last December I had a dream that has bothered me for some time. I was living in a house that had a solid glass front with my husband and our three boys. I was having people into the house; these people were in a panic because of a volcano erupting in back of our house. It was somewhere in the mountains, near the Bay Area.

The eruption was causing fires, and everyone around us was coming to our house."

English-born John Cotton is a concert artist and has gotten a good deal of attention also because of his daring exploits in crossing large oceans on very small crafts. Mr. Cotton is now a resident of Berkeley, California, when he is not at sea. Over the years he has communicated to me a number of recurrent dreams. "I am very high in the air, in the vicinity of Lawrence Bay Bridge, Vancouver, British Columbia. As I watch, a huge wave, 80 to 100 feet high, comes surging down the sound and smashes against the high-rise apartment buildings in West Vancouver with such force that the wave breaks right over the apartment buildings." Mr. Cotton has dreamed this particular dream three times.

Another dream, which so far he has experienced only once, is even more disturbing. "I am a thousand feet over the Salton Sea in southern California and am able to see that the Gulf of California has run right up into the Salton Sea, making that sea become the headwaters of the Gulf." John Cotton remarked in his report to me that he knew a young girl in Vancouver, British Columbia, who had also had a dream in which she saw herself struggling to hold on to her parents who were being swept away by a huge surge of water.

Mr. Cotton's dream visions do come true. An example that seems particularly interesting is reported by him as follows:

In 1966 and '67 I crossed the Pacific in a small yacht by myself. I was making very poor time and began to run out of food. I had a very strong feeling that before I was completely out of food, more food would be brought to me. I visualized a Russian whaler very vividly, and thought that this would be my source of food. I was down to one tin of meat and two tins of vegetables when I sighted a small ship ahead. It altered course toward me. It was a Canadian vessel, escorting the race yachts from Vancouver Island to the Hawaiian Islands. They passed alongside and asked me if I needed any food. After they had passed me some supplies and departed, I went below to note in my log and list the supplies. I had been below for about thirty minutes when there was a loud blast on a siren. I popped my head out of the hatch just as a Russian whaler swept past. The crew on deck were roaring with laughter, probably thinking that they had caught me napping. It was my whaler, the one that I had visualized, complete with rust streaks and Cyrillic writing.

Nick Lambos is a highly respected teacher of ballroom dancing in Tennessee. Within the last six years he has experienced certain happenings he cannot account for by rationalization alone. "One night I had a very unusual dream. All through the night I heard a voice calling, like an echo, 'Art Baker.' Then there was a marquee with this name spelled out in large lights. This went on all night. The next morning I went into the living room to have coffee with my wife, and I said, 'Who in the world is Art Baker? I kept hearing his name called all night long.' She said she didn't know. So I sat down to have my coffee and read the paper. As I was thumbing through, I found a small write-up stating that Art Baker had died. He was the man who used to have a television show called *You Asked For It.*"

But the dream that really bothered Mr. Lambos occurred to him four times:

Recently I have been dreaming about a large earthquake, meaning a very bad one. One time it happened in Nashville, and the other times I couldn't tell where it was. But I saw all downtown buildings fall, stores where my wife and I shop. Also hundreds of people walking down the street to the edge of the city. I have dreamed this several times. Now this week I have dreamed about a horrible flood and tidal wave. This particular dream has happened three times. I have dreamed my wife and I were sitting in front of a large window, like a picture window, having cocktails, and there were other people in the room. All of a sudden from out of nowhere a giant wave came pounding against the window. The water seemed to rise fast and furiously. Finally it broke the glass and we started toward the door. As we opened the door, it poured in, but we made it out. The only thing that bothers me is the fact that the large room we were sitting in seemed to be up high, like on the tenth or twelfth floor, because in my dream we were looking out the window and had a pretty view. In another dream before this one, my little girl and I were out driving, and we came to a bridge and looked at the water getting higher and higher. Then it came up over the bridge and went into this town—I don't recall if it was Nashville or not. The earthquake dreams have been occurring on and off about six or seven years.

Two semiprofessional mediums, Mrs. Dorothy Barrett and Mrs. Virginia Hill of Cincinnati, Ohio, have made predictions from time to time that the local newspapers snap up eagerly. Among their published long-range predictions are earth upheavals that will cause buildings in New York and San Francisco to topple over. "I see it too clearly for it not to happen," Mrs. Barrett is quoted as saying. She also predicts that there will be only one world religion by the year 2000, which makes me wonder who will be left to pray if all the catastrophes predicted for our earth do take place as foreseen. I am not saying that these predictions are merely fear symbols born of an uncertain age and coming from people who may have personal

problems of an entirely different kind to work out. I am convinced that much of what the psychics have foreseen will take
place, while other parts of the predictions will not. I think that
it is nature's peculiar way of letting us work out our own destinies to mix genuine predictions of the future with mere warnings, so that we may still change the course of events if we try
hard enough. Whatever the outcome, it is remarkable that so
many different people, who have no knowledge of each other,
should come up with parallel material. It is something we must
ponder and wonder about, at the same time displaying neither
panic nor ridicule for those who sincerely accept warnings of
this kind as a special talent nature has given them.

A certain number of prophetic dreams involving catastrophes yet to come perhaps can be explained as resulting from
the dreamer's anxiety about the future of the land. This is, however, less easy to accept when the dream, or the person having the vision, has an established track record as a psychic.

It would be easy to ascribe all such dreams and visions to
the results of widely read prophecy accounts from the past,
prophecies made by the great prophets of yesteryear—those
with proven records of having made specific predictions already
come true. But that would make the question of prophecy even
more complex, just as the question of what will come true and
what will not cannot be so easily answered.

CHAPTER 9

Breakthroughs in Medicine

Nothing is more fervently sought than cures for the scourges still afflicting mankind, notably cancer, AIDS, and heart disease, and though much work is going on all the time, no one can for sure predict the outcome—objectively.

It is therefore interesting to note that the question brought forth some very precise answers. When a psychic queried also happens to be a highly qualified physician, then the prognostication takes on the aura of exciting news, albeit a little ahead of its time. When Dr. N. of California originally spoke to me about a cure for a cancer that would be found in the 1970s and of a "Dr. Martin" connected with it, there was no knowledge of this available to either him or me.

Several years later, his prediction had already materialized in part. According to *Hospital Tribune* (March 23, 1970), a new vaccine, called "BCG," had been successfully employed to cause regression in melanoma, one of the more common cancers in humans. "The group was led by Dr. Donald L. Morton, senior investigator at the National Cancer Institute Surgery branch." "Martin" and "Morton" are close enough. How could Dr. N. have known this long before the group got started on the work? He could not have, of course, except through ESP.

Do you foresee any breakthroughs in medicine, and what will these be? What disease will be involved and in what way?

Carolyn Chapman:

"There will be a new discovery for cancer. Definitely. There will be a new discovery and it is coming very soon. It will come from a very simple weed in the forest."*

How soon?

"Probably this year."

For all cancers?

"All cancers. Makes no difference whether it's a bad cancer, or just what sort of a cancer it is."

Virginia Cloud:

"A cure of or adequate treatment of the common cold will be found. The cause and cure of cancer, I feel, will be discovered by one person (man or woman), by a kind of Dr. Salk. I feel strongly that cancer is closely related to the emotions, even to sex, to that part of us that is *life*. The discovery will lead to other answers, long a mystery."

Betty Dye:

"The greatest medical breakthrough will come soon—the cancer cure. Of course, 'everything' will continue to be transplanted. This will soon become a normal procedure, just as removal of tonsils."

John Gaudry:

"I see the initial of a man again—*M, R, M, S*—something like this. I see initials, the first one is very clear. Then I see an *H*, again, and a *J*. This is somebody that's living at the moment. I

---

*A Canadian experimental anti-cancer extraction from organic raw herbs called Flor-Essence, based on Ojibwa Indian tribal medicine, has shown remarkable results in the fight against all kinds of cancer.

feel a sunny climate. There is going to be somebody with these initials that will be making a tremendous discovery. I think this has already happened, actually. It is a very common sort of thing, common—and it is around me at the moment, but there's nothing being done about it. This seems to be a person who is in a very high position."

Jimmy Jacobs:

"I predict that the breakthroughs in medicine will be a direct result of the discoveries in moon dust and the diseases involved will be cancer mainly, which will be completely curable, and I also feel that advances in the causes of coronary will be made and some sort of preventive medicine will be available on the market within a short time. Cancer will be cured. 'Spare part' surgery and banks will be commonplace."

Sybil Leek:

A big breakthrough within five years, with the orthodox medical profession losing its grip on people. Brain implants within ten years by a doctor whose name begins with *YU* (I think it is *YU*, not *Y* and *U*, but cannot be certain about this). Great need for a special type freezing service for all organs of the human body—nothing will be wasted. Major breakthrough in 1975 for paralyzing disease, arteriosclerosis. People are health-conscious today, but it is a pseudo-health thing more related to being 'in' than really regarding health as something wonderful and worth looking after. Such things in the future will be the use of yoga exercises as part of health programs and going back to the healthy mind, healthy body thing."

Bill Linn:

"As we develop vaccines, other viruses will come about that will be stronger than the vaccines that we have developed. I feel that the whole field of parapsychology will be explored, such as the reading of auras, spiritual healing, and people tuning in spiritually with other people, people that are presently in medical institutions, possessed by 'lower entities.' "

Ethel Johnson Meyers:

"Man will not be going in the direction of drugs too long. Natural resources will come again into the fore. It will be a concentration of food or herbs themselves that will heal."

Dr. N.:

"I believe cancer research will win out as we have previously discussed."

Here is what I wrote about Dr. N.'s medical predictions in Predictions: Fact or Fallacy? *in early 1968:*

The doctor also foresees some major discoveries in his own field. A Dr. Martin will discover a cure for cancer in 1971 or 1972, and it will be found that the cancer virus is connected with the *herpes simplex* virus, which appears in common cold sores. Cancer is caused not by this virus, but by the failure of antibodies related to it.

By 1987 he sees clinics testing people for cancer every six months, by inducing a herpetic lesion and then testing it with a serum to see if any cancerous cells are present in the person. After the war, in 1979, cancer research will become more prominent, and there will be many innovations in 1986. One out of three children will be deformed by radiation, and much of the national energy will be directed to research in genetics and embryology.

Julie Parrish:

"I think Dr. Salk is going to discover a cure for cancer."
Why Dr. Salk?

"I just feel it. He's working very hard on something right now. I think he's working on a cancer vaccine, and he'll make it."

John Reeves:

"Well, a breakthrough certainly comes within the next three and a half to four years about the common cold. This is something that I feel sure of. We are going to learn the X-factor, if I may put it that way, involved in what really causes humans to pick up viruses, and I believe that an immunity will be developed within the next three and a half to four years which will greatly control at least 75 percent of the cases of the common cold. The other thing, and I know that I'm disagreeing with other psychics when I say this, but I do not see any breakthrough in cancer at least for seven years; six or seven, let's put it that way."

But you do foresee one then?

"I would say seven years from now there begins a good breakthrough. But that is only a breakthrough. You have to give it another fifteen to twenty years."

Betty Ritter:

"I feel that there will be a cure for cancer, and also something new in heart transplants—something made of plastic."

Shawn Robbins:

"In 1976 there will be a doctor whose name starts with a 'Frazer,' or 'Dr. Azur'; he's an old man with white hair, crewcut type, sticking upwards. Heart transplants will definitely be successful at that time, but it's through this man—it's a new technique that he has. This involves I think ice—it's metal—it's a sheet of metal that I see, it can be put in the body, and it is way below zero. This will enable man to transplant organs without danger of rejection. I see a sheet, light gray metal, definitely ice-cold. Maybe it is not a metal, maybe I just see it as a metal form. This is one of the best things we have—there's no rejection in the transplants with that."

Ms. Robbins predicted further:

"A new law will be passed in the New York State area between 1973 and 1976 making abortions legal.

"In 1971 a replacement to the birth control pill will be found by doctors from Amsterdam or Holland or else the doctors are living in America now, but they are foreign-born.

"Pollution within the next ten years will be the major health concern.

"Cancer in seven years will be treated by a new method called 'R waves' or 'radium waves.' This treatment only controls cancer but does not prevent it.

"In the next ten years a new type of x-ray machine will be developed which doesn't give off harmful radioactive rays. In fact, look forward to new medical machinery that is not powered by radioactives but rather by a new type of energy field."

Fredric Stoessel:

"I think the process of aging is going to be healed to a great degree. There'll be longevity to a much greater degree than we know of now. As a matter of fact, I think that the fear of death is going to be very, very much out. A new attitude toward death will be instituted."

Jill Taggart:

"Cancer will be cured. It is now, but we don't know about it. There is a deadly flu in the making which will strike like the plague, but it will be conquered about a year after its appearance."

Fifteen psychic people participated in this particular experiment. Of the fifteen no fewer than eleven answered in the affirmative regarding a cancer cure within the foreseeable future. Three spoke of a cure for the common cold. It is interesting to recall that Dr. N. mentioned the connection between cold sores (herpes simplex) and a cancer cure back in 1968. In 1970, at a clinic in Port Washington, Long Island, experimental work with an anticancer virus was being conducted on a limited scale with excellent results. The link between the common cold and cancer played an important part in this research, undertaken by the Waldemar Research Foundation.

Today we still have no cure for cancer even though some ways to retard cancer seem to be effective. As I demonstrated in *Healing Beyond Medicine*, the approach of chemotherapy and radiation does not address the cause of the dreaded disease at all. Some remedies derived from natural sources in the rain forests of Costa Rica and Brazil have been effective in the treatment and prevention of some cancers, notably cancers of the male and female reproductive organs.

The prophets of yore did not even mention AIDS. Could it be that some events must remain veiled until a certain point in time has been reached before seers can actually "pick them up" in their psychic visions?

One does not need to be psychic, only view health and healing holistically rather than conventionally, to predict that a totally new concept of what these dread diseases really are is needed and should be acted upon accordingly by the medical establishment, perhaps by incorporating into their methods some of the valid findings and remedies of the alternative schools of medicine.

CHAPTER 10

The Future of the Racial Problem in America

Mark Twain had a saying, "Everybody talks about the weather, but nobody does anything about it." The racial strife in America seems to be somewhat similar. Almost everybody speaks of it, acknowledges that it exists, but very few people actually do anything about it. Today we continue to live in a world fraught with racial polarization; the extremists among black people, on the one hand, demand in militant tones that they be given in a hurry all those rights, privileges, and opportunities they have not had in the past, while, on the other hand, the extreme white fringe wishes to continue denying those same rights, privileges, and opportunities to the blacks. Caught in the middle are those who consider goodwill more important than skin color.

As the turbulent years pass, we find that one fact emerges. It may be that we can't live together, but it may also be that we can't live apart. By the same token, there is no doubt in my mind that the status of race relations in this country must undergo basic changes. Racial strife is a very real threat to the existence of our country. It is a far greater threat, for instance, than foreign involvements are—perhaps not so glamorous from the military point of view, but far more dangerous, since it concerns itself with the heartland of America, with our homes and with our neighbors or would-be neighbors.

The racial problem represents a very major area of concern for anyone in this country. What solution, if any, is found for this problem has direct bearing on the future of not only the country as such but also the safety and well-being of individuals, both black and white. In asking my psychic correspondents to comment upon the question of racial strife, I realized that I might have to look for subtle and involuntary bias in the answers, because even mediums have prejudices. But even if one takes into account the background and individual upbringing of the psychics questioned, there remains enough of a direct ESP nature to deserve inclusion here.

How will racial problems be resolved in America?

Virginia Cloud:

"The racial problem will bring more bloodshed before it is resolved. Eventually we will all come to realize that merely being of any particular ethnic background—be it Caucasian, African-American, Hispanic, or any other race—does not entitle any individual to special privileges. Every individual should be given equal opportunity. This does not mean that every person is equal. To prove oneself through hard work and decent behavior is our American way of life. We have grown on this principle. Anarchy brings only discontent, distrust, and hatred. Its negative force destroys self-respect and ambition. Rugged individualism must and *will* return. Mediocrity will eventually be tossed into the dump heap of discarded passions. We are born alone and we die alone and whatever happiness or success we attain in between results only in what we accomplish alone. Only the predatory animal travels in packs. Man, with his reason, will in time recognize this fact and realize that all professional do-gooders are damn fools."

Betty Dye:

"Strangely enough, a racial change will be partly brought about by the acceptance of spiritualism, psychic research, and so on in our churches and colleges. When man learns and accepts that he is merely one part of a large main body, through healing and love for his fellows, he will think twice before radically inflicting hurt and shame upon 'himself.' Society will finally accept 'himself unto himself.' Romans 13:10—'Love worketh no ill to his neighbor; therefore love is the fulfilling of the law.' "

John Gaudry:

"Well, I don't see it; I don't see this happening somehow, how it is going to be resolved, at all. It's not going to be resolved. Not from within America, that is, but perhaps it will be from without."

Jimmy Jacobs:

"America will try to solve the racial problem by redevelopment of areas and creating new towns with single ethnic populations. This will be a controversial problem and will involve moving people from the slum areas, thus eliminating slums. These people will be moved from the towns and cities most affected by racial problems at very great expense."

Bill Linn:

"We will always have a racial problem. I feel that as long as you have people who are not mentally in tune with others, they do not know what they are doing and you will still have problems. If people would understand the reasons for living, and the reasons of life, I think only in this way can you educate people about the poverty that they are living through, that this might be a karmic reaction for them to live through and to help themselves spiritually by not having the materialistic wealth, but spiritual growth which comes with poverty. I feel that we are going to have a great deal of wars yet. All this ties in together."

Ethel Johnson Meyers:

"Eventually a great understanding will be reached. There will be equality, but oil and water do not mix. This will be a great and long fight, and with it will come an understanding of why one man is white and another man black."

Dr. N.:

"The racial problem will fall back into the background due to the enormous struggle for survival that will be shortly upon us. We will be united by the common bond of conflict."

Julie Parrish:

"I think that it won't resolve itself for a long time. There's going to be a lot of bloodshed before it's solved, and then it will be with the new Aquarian Age people, after the old die-hards have died and then these people will be able to blend."

John Reeves:

"This will be resolved over a period of fifty years. There is going to be a great deal of intermarrying. Also, I don't really foresee any clearing up of the racial problem within the next ten years. I wish people would become more sensible, but it seems to me that things are going the other way at present, and instead of people getting more understanding in this area, I think they are going the other way. I am afraid bigotry is not going to be erased from this country in the next ten years."

Betty Ritter:

"I feel there is going to be a lot of trouble and bloodshed, and this is where Nixon* comes in, as I have predicted before. Police motor units are going to be placed in different parts of the city where there is trouble."

Shawn Robbins:

"At the moment I see this problem, that it will always be the same. It won't get drastically worse, and it's certainly not going to get better. There is no such thing as a solution in the next twenty to one hundred years, or brotherhood between us."

Fredric Stoessel:

"Well, ultimately I think there is going to be intermingling of the races and intermarriage. I have a feeling that there's going to be a horrible, bloody confrontation in the very near future— I think in some of our northern cities, and also somewhere in Texas. After there is this bloody confrontation, I think it will end by intermarriage."

Jill Taggart:

"Remember the Civil War? Race is part of it. Eventually it will have no bearing, but neither you nor I will see that world."

There you have it, not a pretty picture. Of the thirteen psychics queried, ten replied in the negative and only three foresaw a solution of the racial problem within the immediate or at least the foreseeable future. Nine foresaw bloody fights between blacks and whites, even civil war, between the races.

---

*According to H. R. Haldeman's account of the Nixon years given in TV interviews, Nixon is quoted as blaming America's problems on blacks (1994).

PART III

How the Great Prophets See Our Future

CHAPTER 11

The Prophecies of Nostradamus

No documented prophet in relatively recent times has been more detailed, accurate, and of course upsetting to humanity because of the nature of some of his prophecies than Michael Nostradamus, a sixteenth-century French physician and astrologer. Dozens of books have been written about his prophecies, with all kinds of interpretations and translations, many of which are either false or misunderstood. There is also one book by the late Henry Roberts, a New York antiquarian book dealer, who had become so obsessed with his Nostradamus studies that eventually he became convinced that he was, in fact, Nostradamus himself reincarnated! Alas, among the many books discussing Nostradamus's prophecies, Mr. Roberts's is the least reliable. As a matter of fact, the most accurate of all Nostradamus scholars was the late Steward Robb, who passed on just recently. I knew Robb well. He was not only a leading scientific investigator of the paranormal but also a great musicologist and authority on classical composers, such as Richard Wagner, whose works he translated.

I am very confident about Steward's translations and interpretations of the "quatrains," or verses, Nostradamus used to camouflage his prophecies. Those who were sophisticated enough to read between the lines or know what the hints he gave in the verses meant had no great trouble understanding, though some of the hints are still controversial today. The French seer used this camouflage technique because in his time, enlightened Renaissance though it was, it was still not healthy to predict the murder of a king of one's country or the destruction of the papacy in centuries to come. In Spain particularly, but also elsewhere in Catholic Europe, the inquisition was burning anyone daring to have ideas about the future, since clairvoyance was considered witchcraft. Witches, it was thought, had to be destroyed, as they were in league with the devil—the same devil so carefully constructed by a special committee of the church under orders from Pope Innocent III, to find a worthy opponent to Christian theology (and at the same time, by accusing dissenters of worshipping this figment of the church's imagination, doing away with the opposition). There is no "rational" explanation for Nostradamus, and there is no fakery involved. The manuscripts are genuine and readily available to scholars. His first book of prophecies contained some 354 four-line verses expressing his predictions, and several volumes followed. Nostradamus died in 1566, by which time he was held in high repute, or, as Robb put it, "a prophet with honor in his own country."

Nostradamus's prophecies extend from the sixteenth century until the middle of the fourth millennium, and Robb has painstakingly pointed out those that have already been realized. Among other things, Nostradamus foretold the periscope, submarine, airplane, Montgolfier balloon, atomic warfare, and the coming of many wars and events that have become part of history. It would take an entire volume to list them all. During World War II, for example: "An old man with the title of chief will arise, of doddering sense . . . the country divided, conceded to gendarmes."

Marshal Pétain, chief of state, was an old man when the Nazis made him ruler of a portion of divided France—the portion to be ruled by Vichy gendarmes!

It is a scientific axiom that if a large portion of a statement is correct, all of it may well be correct. Every prophecy made by Nostradamus between 1555 and 1566 pertaining to the period between then and today has come true. Not only are his prophecies specific, but they also use terminology completely unknown at the time he made them. Around the middle of the sixteenth century he spoke of communism, aerial bombardments, atom bombs, submarines, and other ideas that came into being only centuries later. He gave the name and profession of the assassin of a French king, an event that transpired in the following century.

There are a total of 942 prophecies. Famed Nostradamus scholar Dr. Alexander Centgraf, a German, has reassembled the deliberately mixed-up chronology of Nostradamus's verses. In 1968 Dr. Centgraf published these verses in their correct sequence. In one of the verses Nostradamus referred to the year 1607, in which the priests would be threatening astronomers because of their discoveries. As a matter of fact, it was in 1607 that a Dutchman by the name of Lippershey invented one of the first telescopes. Shortly thereafter, Galileo Galilei used this new instrument to discover that the earth circles the sun and not vice versa. When he proclaimed this exciting new discovery, he came into conflict with the Church and was eventually forced to recant. But he knew in his heart it was the truth.

Almost 300 years before the planet Neptune was actually discovered, Nostradamus predicted it and referred to the unknown planet by its present name, Neptune. As for our future, Nostradamus predicted a widespread eclipse of the sun in 1999, at which time the French monarchy will be restored following a disastrous war.

Nostradamus prophesied that a great Tartarian warlord will descend on Europe and the Near East in the year 1999. But Erika Cheetham, in *her* interpretation of Nostradamus, connects this prophecy to the Christian millennium syndrome, the medieval belief that at the millennium something terrible will happen to our world. An Arab is believed to be the leader who, backed by fanatic Muslims, unleashes a major war again. It is 1995 as I write this, and it is of course possible that such a person may yet come onto the world scene. But the year A.D. 2000 cannot possibly be meaningful, seeing that Jesus was born seven years earlier than the year 1, as we all know by now. So if the great war were to break out, the year would have to have been 1992, and we know this did not happen.

One of the most noteworthy statements by Steward Robb concerns the validity of all predictions and prophecies, including of course those of the greatest seer of them all, Nostradamus. "Prophecies of disaster and doom that have not yet occurred need never occur," writes Steward Robb. "Any predicted evil can be declared, circumvented, or prevented."

One of the most remarkable of Nostradamus's lines is this one, in Steward Robb's translation: "There will be a head of London from the government of America. . . ." It must be kept in mind that this was written at a time when nobody had heard of a "government of America," when there was no connection between England and America—the first colonists had not yet come here!

I am indebted to John Hogue, today's greatest Nostradamus scholar and author, for his help with a reference I consider of some importance in respect to recent world history.

The terrible nuclear accident that occurred in the Ukraine at Chernobyl atomic plant in 1986 was one of the greatest disasters to befall Europe in decades. Did Nostradamus hint at this event?

In Nostradamus's epistle to King Henry II of France, there is reference to "fiel," which means "bitter" in the French of Nostradamus's time. The line reading "le miel du fiel" likewise could be translated as "the passion or suffering of 'the bitter,'" and the term "bitter" could then be a mask hiding the words "amoise amère," or bitter herb. "Bitter herb of Artemis" is the French term for what we call wormwood or, by extension, absinthe. *Chernobyl* in Russian means "wormwood." Thus, the reference is to future "suffering by wormwood (Chernobyl)." Even more ominous is the mention of *wormwood* in the Apocalypse, the prophecies of St. John; here there is no code, no disguise, and the term is plain. It only made sense, however, after the Chernobyl catastrophe had taken place!

For those who wish to delve into the prophecies of the great Nostradamus themselves, I have included a listing of the principal books dealing with his work. I am sure there are others. No other prophet ever attracted as much attention.

One should study these books with a measure of caution, however. The original text is reliable, but the translations from sixteenth-century French are not always correct, as the French of Nostradamus's time often differs from modern French. Further, as Steward Robb has pointed out, certain terms had specific meaning to Nostradamus, but may have a different meaning to anyone else. For instance, when Nostradamus speaks of "oriental," he does not mean an Oriental but simply a "person from the East"—the east of France, that is.

The most accurate books on Nostradamus are Steward Robb's, and I am happy that his *Nostradamus/And the End of Evils Began* was recently republished by Longmeadow Press. Here are the other books:

Erika Cheetham, *The Prophecies of Nostradamus*

Erika Cheetham, *The Further Prophecies of Nostradamus*

Karl Drude, *Nostradamus.* (This text is in German.)

John Hogue, *Nostradamus and the Millennium.* (This is an excellent reference complete with visuals.)

John Hogue, *The Millennium Book of Prophecy.* (This most recent work by John Hogue is published by Harper Collins and is even better than Hogue's earlier work.)

Frank J. MacHovec, *Nostradamus—His Prophecies for the Future*

Rudolf Putzien, *Nostradamus—Weissagungen ueber den Atomkrieg.* (This text is in German.)

Steward Robb, *Nostradamus and Napoleon*

Steward Robb, *Prophecies on World Events by Nostradamus*

Henry Roberts, *The Complete Prophecies of Nostradamus.* (This text is regarded as controversial.)

Charles A. Ward, *Oracles of Nostradamus.* (This is a very old text.)

My recommendation is that readers concentrate on the books by Steward Robb and John Hogue. It is all in there, and *correctly.*

CHAPTER 12

The "Grand Prophecies": A Hard Look at Our Future

H. G. Wells wrote a remarkable book, which later also became a very impressive motion picture, called *The Shape of Things to Come*. What he foresaw was total destruction of the England he knew and the emergence of a kind of latter-day caveman culture that would last until the survivors of the atomic holocaust that had destroyed England emerged again from hidden centers and took over (thanks to an advanced technology they had meanwhile developed).

These events never took place, of course, but they might have, if the course of human events had run differently. Even so astute a prognosticator as H. G. Wells, right many times, can be wrong. Nineteenth-century novelist Jules Verne predicted the submarine and many other later inventions and events; that was inspired intuition, if you wish, but not prophecy.

But since our future is the only future we have, so to speak, we had better examine very closely and dispassionately the likelihood of certain prophecies of destruction coming true.

It should be remembered that all prophecy relies upon human beings as channels and that people are fallible. Even those who have exhibited the greatest degree of accuracy have on occasion been wrong. The very nature of foretelling the future defies orthodox scientific law. Consequently we cannot be at all sure that we understand the time concept as it exists in that dimension in which prophecy is possible. If these individuals derive their information from a common source that may be not fully understood by us at present, then there must be some form of law governing that source.

The first prophets were the shamans—the witchcraft priests—of the Stone Age communities. It helped to have extrasensory perception in those early days. But even if the ancient shaman foretold the future more in fanciful terms than with a degree of psychic knowledge, he was sufficiently skilled in the use of words to avoid any serious difficulties if the future did not materialize as predicted. Where the shaman was accurate, he was, of course, a highly respected and honored member of the tribe.

Since we do not have written records of any such individuals, we cannot judge how many of them were in fact good mediums. Only when we come to the Mediterranean cultures of the biblical lands and Assyria, Babylonia, and Egypt do we find prophets mentioned by name and accomplishments. In ancient Israel, in particular, prophets were highly respected and often very much feared individuals. They were so powerful at one time that the kings of Israel had to reckon with their influence. In the later years of ancient Israel the kings resumed their unique positions of power, and prophecy was no longer a pursuit open to anyone who felt moved by the spirit. The state preferred that the entire matter of prophecy be channeled in such a way that it could be controlled. There were differences of opinion between prophet and king—Jeremiah, for example, warned his king of impending disaster if he didn't mend his ways. Other public outcries by psychically gifted individuals against the evils of their times are legion in the Old Testament.

Because the ancient prophets did not have to contend with modern scientists and the cool, clinical minds of researchers bent only on establishing validity, they were able to couch their predictions and prophecies in colorful language, sometimes deliberately, sometimes unintentionally. A prophecy turned into a poem has a powerful impact on the listener. On the other hand, a bland, prosaic statement might not have the same emotional appeal. But enough biblical predictions did come true to consider the profession of prophecy a legitimate one with a fair degree of accuracy over the years.

Probably the earliest "grand prophecy" that has come down to us is the Apocalypse, or Revelations of St. John, in which he describes the coming of Armageddon and the destruction of the earth by fire and sword. The "four horsemen of the Apocalypse" indeed present a frightening symbol of future destruction.

In the pagan world prophets were equally admired and feared, by both the rulers and the people. The Delphic Oracle was a very lucrative enterprise for the priests attending it. The priestess sat over a fissure in the earth from whence emanated sulphuric gases. These gases rendered the priestess partially unconscious, very much as a medium is in partial trance when the bonds of consciousness are loosened either by the medium herself or through hypnosis. In this state the priestess was able to foresee future events and give what we call "readings" today. These priestesses of the Delphic Oracle sometimes used ambiguous language—but by no means always. One of the most famous prophecies was the oracle's telling King Croesus: "When you cross the Halys, you will destroy a great empire." Croesus thought the empire to be that of his adversary; in fact it turned out to be his own. In ancient Rome prophecy made use of such unusual things as analysis of the innards of fowl and staring at a sand-covered tablecloth. Soothsayers were frequently right in their predictions. One of the most noteworthy ones concerned Julius Caesar, who was warned to beware of the ides of March. Caesar, unfortunately, wasn't much of a believer in the occult, and the rest is history.

Just as today, people would travel great distances to consult reputable psychics, or soothsayers, in order to learn more about their future or that of the world in which they lived. But with the advent of Christianity all this was changed. The Christian church had Jesus as its intermediary between man and God. Foretelling the future fell into the category of miracles; miracles were the province of God, Jesus and his clergy, but not of ordinary men. A prophet either would have to be a priest or would be accused of heresy or, worse yet, of being in league with the devil. For what was not of God was of the devil, in the eyes of the church.

As the Middle Ages darkened the world, the church looked into the Old Testament and found passages condemning psychic activity. Many of these passages are even today quoted as proof that the bible frowns upon psychics, extrasensory perception, and any other form of divination. This is not so. What the Old Testament referred to were unauthorized prophets, and the passages must be understood in the light of the times in which they were written. At that time there was dissent within Israel, and the government lived in very real fear of some fanatical prophet causing a rebellion by falsely foretelling disaster for the government then in power. It was therefore convenient to condemn all prophets so that the government could be assured no one would rise against it, prophesy, and have the masses on his side. For clearly such an individual was in defiance of the law, both temporal and religious. The Christian church, however, referred to these passages frequently out of context and used them to suppress any and all psychic activity. If any man felt compelled to prophesy, he had to do so quietly and privately. If caught, he would have been condemned to death. The church did not permit any other spiritual development than that which was possible within its rigid doctrine and law.

There has never been an age in the development of mankind and history where prophets did not speak. Today, they are free and safe to do so without fear of being accused of witchcraft or complicity with the devil. Not so long ago, such freedom would not have been possible, and prophecy was allowed and accepted only so long as it worked within the framework of the current state religion, whether Judaism, Christianity, or any other faith. While this inevitably inhibited the prophets somewhat, they found ways to tell the truth (as they saw it) without offending authorities. In short, they found ways to get the message across to the world.

St. Odile, the patron saint of Alsace, born in A.D. 657, is considered the source of a prophecy relating to a "bellicose Germany" and a "conqueror starting from the banks of the Danube who will win victories on land, by sea, and even in the air. This prophecy goes on to describe World War II in detail. Whether this prophecy really stems from the seventh century saint or is a later medieval prophecy attributed to her, it is definitely of very ancient origin.

Mother Shipton, who lived around 1488, liked to couch her prophecies in rhyme and verse. While some of her prophecies are open to varied interpretations, some are quite clear. Here is an example: "Carriages without horses shall go/and accidents fill the world with woe/around the earth thoughts shall fly/in the twinkling of an eye."

Perhaps the greatest seer in our time was Edgar Cayce whose record of prophecies is obtainable from the Association for Research and Enlightenment, Virginia Beach, Virginia, where the headquarters of the Cayce Foundation is located.

Cayce passed away in 1945, but there are three books dealing with this extraordinary man in great detail—Thomas Sugrue's *There Is a River*, Gina Cerminara's *Many Mansions*, and Jess Stearn's *The Sleeping Prophet*.

Cayce's medical readings transformed this simple photographer's life into an astounding psychic career, and his prophecies concerning the earth are no less overwhelming. It must be remembered that Edgar Cayce had no scientific training or special knowledge whatever, yet in trance was able to describe accurately conditions that were far beyond his comprehension while awake.

Some of Cayce's prophecies concerning the future of our planet are worth keeping in mind. All of them were on file at Virginia Beach prior to 1945.

Cayce prophesied that between 1958 and 1998 California's coastline would be changed, most of Japan would disappear into the sea, new land would rise off the American east coast, and the Arctic and Antarctic regions would turn tropical. The upheaval would start in the South Pacific, he averred, while on the opposite side of the globe there would be heavy disturbances centering around Mount Etna, Sicily.

In 1944, Edgar Cayce predicted that in "another generation" New York City would disappear, but that other areas, such as portions of California, Georgia, and Carolina would go even sooner. Ohio, Indiana, Illinois, and parts of Canada were the areas he deemed safest.

Because of Nostradamus and Cayce and their dire prophecies of catastrophes and changes to come, a lot of people, not just true believers, are scared. Did Cayce know of Nostradamus's prophecies and did they influence his own? Possible but not likely. So when both prophets sound a similar alarm about the future, they might be drawing on the same source, but individually, thus reinforcing the validity, and even the *probability*, of the events to take place.

Cayce predicted that between 1968 and 1998 Los Angeles, San Francisco, and New York would be hit by major destruction. While this has unfortunately come to pass in the case of the two California cities, it is more unlikely with regard to New

York. Although Manhattan rests on a deep fault in the earth, it is a fault quite unlike the California fault lines.

The end of Communism and the United States and Russia becoming allies and friends was an unlikely situation when Cayce stated it, but of course it has come to pass. Christianization and democratization of Red China, also foreseen by Cayce, is yet to come, but the rising of Atlantis, the lost continent, while a reality to many, has not yet shown any sign of happening, especially by the date set by Cayce.

Just as with Nostradamus, whose prophecies I take very seriously, I regard Cayce's with respect. However, I find troublesome the fatalistic position of people accepting these dire predictions as inevitable. The higher level of destiny places any one of us at a place and in a time where we are meant to be. Time as we know it is only a convenience and not an absolute. Certainly it is nonexistent in the dimension beyond this one. The power of prayer and spiritual renewal can and will influence the outcome of events, though we cannot really know which prophecy will be fulfilled as made and which may yet be averted. That, too, is part of the karmic system, to encourage our efforts toward preventing evil and destruction in our world.

Taken by orthodox scientific standards, prophecy of specific events that lie in the future is impossible. The order of the universe as we know it completely excludes even the possibility of foreknowledge so long as specific details are involved. Vague generalizations and educated guesses by well-trained observers do not fall into this category, of course. I am referring to very detailed and clearly defined events, possibly with dates and names of those to be involved. Such foreknowledge cannot be accepted by the orthodox scientist, and for good reason. Knowing events before they come to pass is in direct conflict with the nature of time and space as scientists know it. But there seems to be a second order, superior to the order of cause and effect. The well-known psychiatrist Carl Jung, in a book of great significance called *Acausal Synchronicity, or the Law of Meaningful Coincidence,* demonstrated the existence of this order. Much of the so-called coincidence in our lives can be examined from an entirely different point of view, one of inter-relationship on an inner plane.

The question of fate, free will, and destiny is closely linked with the nature of time and space. If a person can foresee future events in detail, perhaps involving individuals who have not been born or who are as yet totally beyond the horizon of the individual involved, then something larger than the accepted rational order of things must be in operation. If events can indeed be foreseen at a distance in time or space or both, these events must already exist in a dimension other than the one we are used to. If there is such a dimension, then there must be someone or some law organizing the sequence of events. I have often referred to the "boys upstairs" who supervise the higher order of things. Whether one wishes to take the religious path or to explain life as a natural sequence of interrelated events, the fact remains that fate exists. There are events in existence independent of us. When we as indi-viduals approach these events, we become aware of them. Depending upon our reactions, we will take one of several paths leading away from each particular event. In turn, we will face other events on this path. We will have the privilege of choosing how to react to each and every event facing us. Thus destiny is neither a fixed fate nor free will, but a combination of both.

CHAPTER 13

The Vatican Prophecies

The power of the popes has always been shrouded in a kind of mystery, just as the "divine right of kings" has for many centuries kept rulers of sometimes doubtful qualifications in power.

On a realistic level, the pope is nothing more than the head of the Roman Catholic church, a man, inspired perhaps, but not a miracle worker. And yet, the enormous energies stemming from the religious faith of millions of people have endowed the papacy with almost supernatural status. No other head of a religious community shares that unique reputation, except perhaps the chief rabbi of some Hasidic sects believed by his followers to be the real Messiah.

Thus it is not surprising that the prophets have commented upon the fate of the papacy for centuries. In the Middle Ages the popes were also temporal rulers—contrary to Jesus' kind of Christianity—and only in modern times have the popes of Rome retreated to their spiritual sanctuaries, where their position is unchallenged.

In the '90s, the fate of the papacy is of less impact than it might have been five hundred years ago, but its destiny, while no longer of geopolitical importance, has tremendous spiritual and moral implications for millions of people. In the following pages I present precise prophecies regarding the Vatican and certain popes. There are amazing similarities among them, suggesting, at the very least, a common "source."

St. Malachy was a medieval abbot whose prophecies of doom foretold the end of the Vatican some eight hundred years ago—giving a description of every pope elected since that time. The reign of John Paul I was characterized as "of the waxing moon," and indeed his reign lasted just about that long— thirty-four days. John Paul II is referenced to in the Malachy prophecies as "of the eclipse of the sun," and a more dramatic description of the Communist world can hardly be given from the church's point of view!

Malachy warns us that only three more popes remain before the Holy See vanishes at the death of Peter II, and Michael Nostradamus, the famous sixteenth-century prophet, predicted the end of the Vatican in our time.

Jan Cornelius van der Heide lives in a small town in the Netherlands. He is about forty-five years old, is married, and makes his living as an artist and sometime poet. From time to time, van der Heide has had visions about future events, many of which have already come true, like the time he woke up and "saw my father with hands and face covered with blood, his head had gone through a pane of glass . . . his car totally wrecked." Two months later, the accident occurred, but being forewarned, the elder van der Heide somehow survived.

Jan van der Heide claims that a long-dead monk inspires his many religious paintings, which have a strange, ethereal quality to them. Perhaps because of his religious orientation, van der Heide was chosen to warn the world on September 13, 1978, that the newly elected Pope John Paul I "would not live long, but would die within four months." A friend of van der Heide's reported: "On Saturday, September 16, 1978 I visited van der Heide's family. That evening, after Jan had read to us one of his poems about religion, he suddenly said, 'Pope John Paul will die suddenly within four months.' "

As the weeks passed, van der Heide felt more and more that the tragic event was not far off. On September 28, he decided to write to me, to reiterate his concern about John Paul I. That letter, sent off the following day, reached me several days later. But on the same afternoon that the letter was mailed, September 29, Pope John Paul I suddenly passed away.

No sooner had a new pope been elected than Jan van der Heide's second sight tuned in on him: "John Paul II will be involved in an airplane accident in a southern country, perhaps South America. It will be near dry, arid land with rocky soil and coast . . . the figures 1 and 8 suggest the year 1981."

According to the Dutch seer, the new pope would show himself very orthodox and unyielding in matters of doctrine. Van der Heide wrote this on October 19, 1978. By now it has become clear he was right; the new pope's unyielding stand on celibacy has already been made known. Van der Heide predicts that because of John Paul II's stand, more splinters will occur in the church. Polarization will become more pronounced.

According to the Malachy prophecy, the pope following John Paul I would come "from the eclipse of the sun"—an apt description of the Iron Curtain country Poland. Apparently, the impact of what may well have been a fated event was so strong it penetrated the unconscious, psychic level of several other people. Bohdan Zacharko is a tool-and-die-maker of Ukrainian descent, now living in Connecticut. On August 27, 1978, during Mass, he suddenly had a vision. "I saw two coffins," he explained to me, "one opened and the other closed. . . . I seemed to be standing in front of the Vatican. I knew that the open coffin held John Paul I, but I could not see anything further of the closed coffin, except to the right I saw the towers of Moscow. From this I received the feeling that John Paul I would live only for a short while, and that his successor would not be Italian but Polish. I shared my vision with my coworkers and my family, but everyone laughed at me."

Edith Filliette has had ESP experiences all her life but never thought too much of them. Two years ago, however, she began to write them down as they occurred.

Educated in Europe and Canada, Ms. Filliette worked as a writer for *Readers Digest* and is now a direct-mail promotion consultant, making her home in Massachusetts. In late July or early August, she had a "vivid dream," which left her very puzzled at the time.

"I was walking down a busy street somewhere in Europe, looking for transportation to 'the other side of town.' I asked a woman passerby for directions. 'I know of a shortcut, but you must pass through the Polish Embassy,' she replied. At the Polish Embassy I noticed a grand marble stairway winding up to another floor. I glanced upwards and saw three Catholic cardinals in full regalia coming down the stairway. I thought it strange and at the same time I felt they were cardinals from Poland and had come to the embassy for some official papers. Two of the cardinals passed me without a look in my direction. But the third one stopped and looked straight at me as if he were trying to convey a message. He was very close, and I could see his face very distinctly. He was an attractive man of between fifty and sixty, clean-shaven, with light or gray hair slightly protruding beneath the biretta, with a dignified and strong appearance. After some seconds of staring at me, he turned away and continued his walk downstairs, and I continued through the Polish Embassy, walking up the marble stairs, then through a long corridor, until I reached the 'other side of town.' There the dream ended."

As soon as news of the death of Pope Paul VI reached the world, Ms. Filliette told two friends that the next pope might be Polish, and she described him. However, when John Paul I, an Italian, was elected she had a very strong feeling that a mistake had been made. Soon she was to learn how right she had been.

"The day John Paul I died," she explained, "I was hospitalized at the Massachusetts General Hospital in Boston. I did not know the pope had died during the night, and I was sitting up that particular morning around 6:45 A.M. Suddenly I heard an inner voice urging me, 'Turn on your TV . . . something important has happened.' I rejected the idea, as I have an aversion to watching TV. But the voice returned, more insistent. 'Turn to channel 5 and see what happened. . . .' I finally did, and there on the screen was Pope John Paul I and the announcement of his sudden death. At that moment I felt my dream had taken on meaning and that the next pope would indeed be Polish and that he would be elected on October 16. I said so to a friend." Ms. Filliette's strange encounter with the unknown was not over by any means. Since she has no interest in Poland, nor any Polish relatives, she knew nothing about Polish cardinals. When the new pope was elected on October 16—just as she had predicted—she was shocked to recognize his face; it was indeed the face she had seen so vividly in her dream months before!

Ms. Filliette's witnesses are her husband, a priest, and a business executive. Their names are known to me. There is no doubt about the truth and dates of Ms. Filliette's amazing prophecies. Edith Filliette saw three cardinals in her dream: Poland does indeed have three cardinals. But more ominous seems the connection with St. Malachy's prophecy: three more popes—the present one and two more—then the church will come to an end. A Dutch seer . . . a Connecticut tool-and-die-maker . . . a Massachusetts copywriter . . . and who knows who else. Do they have a pipeline to the future?

CHAPTER 14

The Prophecies of
Jan van der Heide

I first heard about Jan Cornelius van der Heide in the fall of 1978 and got to meet him in person the following year. He offered to put me up in his little house in Oegstgeest, a town halfway between Amsterdam and Leyden. Then as now, the bearded, jovial, kindhearted man was known locally as a *parag-nost*, a psychic, even though he made his living primarily as a journalist and artist. With his lovely wife Ans, he lived a pleasant life trying to advance the cause of genuine parapsychology, helped publish a magazine about it, and gradually became well known in the Netherlands as a prophet.

Like all prophets, some of his predictions come true and some do not, a very puzzling thing to explain. But Jan's prophecy about Pope John Paul I is so uncanny, and so well documented, as I explained in the previous chapter, that one expects the majority of his visions to come true. When they do, they are startlingly similar to what Jan had predicted, but there are also many prophecies that have not occurred, though some may yet happen.

Could it be that such detailed ominous prophecies as Jan's

195

description of World War III and Russian attacks on the West were actually in the minds, even the planning stage of some people in the East? Obviously, this prediction never came to pass and could not come to pass unless a new, belligerent Soviet Union were to rise in what could only be a distant future, practically speaking. But that is really unlikely, so I must conclude that the prophet saw what *may* have been a thought pattern or a warning manufactured by spiritual forces to induce humanity to work together, possibly also triggered to some extent by the pervasive fear of Soviet intentions in the 1970s, which many Europeans harbored.

I am presenting van der Heide's World War III prophecy, nevertheless, because it is so startlingly detailed. Beginning with August 15, 1975, van der Heide had a series of spectacular psychic previews of things to come—things destined to happen unless America did something about them. According to Jan van der Heide, the Soviets have been planning a *blitzkrieg*, a surprise attack against Western Europe all the while they are signing arms limitation pacts and other soothing agreements with the West. The Dutch seer claims that Russian bunkers are already in existence along the borders leading to West Germany, via Austria, Czechoslovakia, Hungary, and especially near certain cities, which he pinpoints as Sopron, Hungary, Bratislava, Zuvgno, Asch, and Kisalfoeld, and in the Bohemian forest—all inside Czechoslovakia and all controlled by the Russian military.

"Everywhere there are disguised bunkers containing gas," van der Heide says. "These are meant for chemical and gas warfare—one type of gas is heavily radioactive and causes death by destroying the red blood corpuscles."

The Dutch prophet sees the Soviet advantage in huge fleets of troop-carrying helicopters equipped with atomic weapons. There already exist, according to van der Heide's visions, factories in Warsaw Pact countries that are in reality not factories but staging areas for military personnel and material. From there, swarms of helicopters will eventually attack South Germany and Austria. Russia does not worry about China; the principal targets can be covered with atom bombs. Also, the Russians already have tactical atomic weapons at the border with China, twelve atomic canons directed toward Peking.

Van der Heide's visions come to him unsought, usually just as he goes to sleep or when he wakes up. Some pictures appear to him as accomplished facts, others are more vague, as if the events are still in the formative stages. But van der Heide is emphatic in his contention that if the West takes strong countermeasures, the terrible visions may never become reality or at least not to the extent he sees them roll by his psychic eye.

But fleets of helicopters are not the only surprise the Russians have in store for the West. Entire divisions of Russian soldiers will be dressed in American, British, French, German, and Austrian uniforms. Some of them will speak English. Chaos on the battlefield is the intention due to the defenders' inability to know who is friend and who is foe. Even Western model tanks will be copied by the Russians, and only the Russians will know which ones are really theirs, thanks to an electronic signal apparatus built into their copies of Western tanks. At present, these tanks are being stored underground.

On the other hand, says Jan van der Heide, the Russians have developed an antitank weapon that can be fired by one soldier. Three rockets leave the gun at the same moment, and its accuracy is truly devastating. The rockets contain radiation gas. If the rocket does not explode, the crew is killed by radiation within five hours of contact, as the rays penetrate metal.

Of course, all is not perfect for the Russians either, says van der Heide. The dire events he foresees are still a few—perhaps as much as three—years away. At the moment, the Russians have difficulties with their long-range rockets, the guiding mechanism does not work well, nor is the fuel adequate. Their medium-range and short-distance rockets are more accurate, thus the danger to European cities is now greater.

In the years ahead, Russia is planning a surprise attack against Western Europe. Just prior to this time, Russian influence in Scandinavia will increase, and Finland will be drawn into the Russian orbit. Soviet submarines will appear more and more in northern waters and a special apparatus will be placed on the ocean floor by them, to confuse Western radar—this is a newly developed weapon.

Jan van der Heide warns of fifth columns already in place in important centers of West Germany, especially at Kaiserslautern, Bonn, Karlsruhe, Sued Limburg, and Essen. Under the guise of wanting to unite West and East Germany, Russia intends seizing all Germany. When the attack occurs, the Western powers will try to prevent World War III by making an accommodation with the invader, and part of West Germany will be given up. The greatest battles will take place in the German high plateau area and northwestern Austria.

"Can we prevent all this from happening?" I asked the Dutch seer.

"If the West will greatly increase its espionage and surveillance especially in the border areas," van der Heide replied, "the surprise effect of the attack will be gone. The Russians have to be told that their plans are known." Just how reliable a prophet is Jan van der Heide? I wondered. But van der Heide's psychic predictions so far have been ominously accurate.

- On September 16, 1978, he wrote in his diary that Pope John Paul I would live less than four months. The Pope died September 29, 1978.

- He warned his father that he had seen him with blood-covered face and hands, because his head had gone through a pane of glass during an automobile accident, and that the car would be a total wreck. Two months later, the accident occurred exactly as foreseen.

- On October 19, 1978, van der Heide stated to me in writing that a new oil crisis was about to happen. By early 1979, Iran's oil crisis was in full force.

Mr. van der Heide by no means considers himself solely a prophet of doom. "I want to warn the world what *may* happen if they don't pay attention to the secret preparations now going on behind the Iron Curtain," he says. "If West Germany and Austria are properly fortified and protected, world peace may be preserved. But President Carter's human rights campaigns, and the dissident movement in the East are likely to force the hands of the Kremlin leaders to take drastic action sooner."

Jan Cornelius van der Heide of Holland is by no means the only psychic warning of Russian invasion plans for Western Europe. World War III, starting in West Germany, was predicted in greatest detail by a Black Forest farmer, Alois Irlmaier, as long as thirty years ago. Another native prophet, a fisherman named Anton Johansson, and several other grassroots prophets of Western Europe said pretty much the same things many years ago.

If great events cast their shadows ahead of them, are people like Jan Cornelius van der Heide privileged to preview them and in doing so, give mankind a last chance to escape its terrible future? "I am not a political person," says van der Heide. "I only want the world to know that *there is still time.* Still time to do something about my visions." Jan van der Heide has registered prophecies with me from time to time, with the postmark guaranteeing the proper time reference. A great deal of this material refers mainly to Holland and people and situations with little impact on the world at large. But a good deal is also relative to international conditions, and a great deal of it never came to pass, at least not in our time. Still, there are some interesting predictions, and I will list them here.

NOVEMBER 23, 1980: "Someone will shoot at Reagan."

SEPTEMBER 2, 1989: "The Berlin Wall will come down." Witnessed by radio journalist Marion Dietrich, originally from East Germany.

NOVEMBER 18, 1989: "People will try to kill Gorbachev."

NOVEMBER 18, 1990: "There will be a short and heavy war in the Middle East: I see American bombers above Baghdad."

NOVEMBER 18, 1990: "Limited use of nerve gas by Iraq."

NOVEMBER 18, 1990: "Gorbachev will disappear from the scene in 1991. We will soon be able to read his memoirs."

JANUARY 18, 1991: "Arafat will speak about peace with Israel in a short time.

Some of these were also broadcast by Radio Veronica in the Netherlands.

FEBRUARY 19, 1993: "Unsuccessful attack by shooting on President Clinton."

FEBRUARY 19, 1993: "British and United States aircraft over Yugoslavia in March and April of 1993."

OCTOBER 11, 1993: "Civil war in Russia."

It is perhaps reassuring to see that even a very excellent prophet like van der Heide can be wrong about disaster as often as he is right.

CHAPTER 15

The Outstanding
Prophets of Today

There is a great deal of difference between a talented psychic predicting future events to individual clients and a gifted individual making world predictions, prophecies, spontaneously and to no one in particular. Those who are witness to such prophecies will vouch for them, but the true prophecy comes unsought and usually as a surprise to the practitioner of the psychic arts. The source for such material is uncertain, whether at the deeper level of the prophet's own consciousness or emanating from a spirit communicator or guide inspiring the prophet with the material. What counts is the quality of the prophecy, the track record of the prophet in respect to past prophecies having actually come true, and of course the likelihood of the prophecy being fulfilled at some point in time.

Many books have been published about prophets and prophecy—some good, some less so, some from an enlightened scientific point of view, some imbued with religious or metaphysical enthusiasm. An analogy is appropriate here: There are millions upon millions of people driving cars. Some are truly brilliant at it, many are terrible and cause accidents, and the majority lie between those extremes. So it is with prophets. There are very few truly great ones, and even the few that do exist are far from completely right all the time. It appears that the will of the powers that be is to give us a little leeway to doubt the terrible events prophesied, and yet warn us about them sufficiently so that we may take heed, and action, to change the outcome.

No doubt there are outstanding prophets alive and active today of whom I know nothing. The ones I will touch upon here are people whose work I have been familiar with for a long period of time. I feel that I am able to judge the accuracy of their predictions.

Apart from the Dutch seer Jan Cornelius van der Heide, about whom I have written in the two previous chapters, there are three people I respect as modern prophets. Their prophecies were never sought out by tabloid reporters. No, these ladies—and it so happens they are all women—called me to confide their prophecies in the hope that I could warn the world in some fashion and thus help prevent the outcome, if the prophecy was of a dire nature. It is true that I have certain high-level connections with government and have communicated such warning prophecies immediately when I felt they were to be taken seriously. Nobody can be sure as to which prophecies are warnings, and subject to alteration by human will or action, and which are in fact only previews of certain things to come. It is therefore unwise to allow oneself to panic at a predication that, while prophesied by a serious prophet, may nevertheless not come to pass. If it does indeed occur, the person worried about it may find himself far from the disaster, perhaps because destiny so wanted it in his case!

Having said this, I will present here some of the prophecies communicated to me, and in some instances to other witnesses at the time, regarding situations and events affecting a great many people.

Rosanna Rogers, of Cleveland and New York City, is a remarkably gifted professional psychic reader, whose knowledge of the tarot cards far exceeds that of any other tarot specialist, living or dead. Then, too, Rosanna uses some 220 cards of her own inimitable design, whereas everybody else uses the traditional seventy-eight cards.

Now and again, Rosanna has a flash of prophecy, which she communicates to me and to other witnesses. Should the event predicted occur, she reminds one and all of her prophetic statements.

Rosanna Rogers is in her later middle years. She was born in Austria and brought up in Germany, where she attended high school at the Convent of the Sisters of St. Francis in Pirmasens, and college at the Convent of San Lioba, in Freiburg. She lives in a colorful house in one of Cleveland's quiet districts, on Svec Avenue, and has her own local cable television program. But people from many parts of the world keep reaching out to her for predictions.

Over the years, Rosanna has sent me predictions or made them in my presence or to reputable witnesses who have testified accordingly. Here are some of the most outstanding, relating primarily to world affairs.

Dateline January 10, 1990: "I see a 707 airplane, approaching the Atlantic coast, crashing. I perceive digits . . . 5?"

January 26, 1990: Colombian airliner, Flight 52, a 707, crashes near New York City.

Dateline September 23, 1983: "The United States and the Soviet Union will recognize the need to work together in unison as the danger comes from nations with nothing to lose, such as Iran, Iraq, and Libya."

June–July 1990: The U.S. and Soviet Union chummy as never before, and worries about Iraq and Iran greater than ever.

Dateline July 19, 1973: "Nixon may get out of the Watergate affair elegantly by resigning."

August 7, 1973: Nixon resigns.

During the summer of 1989, Rosanna, whom I had been monitoring carefully as to her accuracy for thirteen years, insisted that all was not well with the president and his family. She was certain that there were health problems and that we would hear about them soon, along with other problems even more worrisome, concerning his immediate family! Finally on January 10, 1990, she put her concerns in writing to me. How accurate was all this?

On February 15, 1990, Barbara Bush went through surgery on her lip and dealt with an eye problem; on January 29, 1990, Neil Bush, the president's son, started having serious business problems still mounting to ominous proportions, and on April 12, 1990, the president himself discovered signs of an early glaucoma problem.

For a European-born woman with horrible memories of the Hitler area, predicting the innocence of a man accused as a concentration camp guard and war criminal necessitated putting professional integrity above deep feelings. But Rosanna Rogers did just that. While all the world knew that a man named Demjanjuk, deported by the United States, was being tried in Israel for his life, because he had been identified by witnesses as "Ivan the Terrible," a particularly vicious and murderous concentration camp guard, nobody much doubted the outcome. But Demjanjuk and his lawyer insisted all along that he was not the man and that he was being wrongfully accused. Was it really a case of mistaken identity? On January 10, 1990, Rosanna Rogers stated to me that "the Demjanjuk case will get a new twist; they've got the wrong man." Personally, I doubted it, but events proved me wrong and the Cleveland psychic right.

February 26, 1990: Polish villagers who live near the former Treblinka concentration camp tell reporters for the television program *Sixty Minutes* that the man dubbed "Ivan the Terrible" was really named Marczenco, not Demjanjuk.

February 28, 1990: Ohio congressman J. Trafficant, in whose district the accused man had lived for many years, takes up his case in Congress.

May 14, 1990: The Israeli court hears an appeal from the man's death sentence imposed by a lower court. As a result, the Demjanjuk case is reopened. A new investigation by the court set the man free. He now lives quietly back in Cleveland.

Going from the very serious to the very superficial: Rosanna stated to me through 1988 and 1989 that millionaire Donald Trump was heading for a fall. Then on January 10, 1990, she put it this way: "He will learn the raw fear of losses, both emotionally and in business, but he will bounce back." On the same day, Rosanna assured me that former President Reagan would be the first president in American history to testify in court. He did, in February and March.

As of June 1994, Rosanna foresees more trouble in the world, emphasizing that it is the small nations "with nothing to lose" that present nuclear threats—Iran, Iraq, and Libya in particular. (Not a word about North Korea, though.) In the Middle East, she prophesies a major conflict involving several countries, sometime before 1999. And in the United States, she predicts "open warfare in the streets" and "tax revolt" by the citizens.

Yolana Lassaw, usually called by only her first name (which is actually her mother's and which she adopted for good luck years ago), is today the leading deep-trance medium in America. In the tradition of Eileen Garrett, Ethel Johnson Meyers, and Trixie Allingham, to name but a few of those I have worked with over the years, Yolana makes her living as a psychic reader available to clients for consultations about their private lives and future.

She has also become a busy adjunct to the police, giving freely of her time in the investigations of murder cases and missing persons in particular. I have taken part in some of these journeys, and she is truly on target.

Now and again Yolana has prophetic visions. She communicates these to me, as we have been close friends and associates in this work for twenty years. Here are some of Yolana's prophecies and the outcomes.

On November 1, 1978, Yolana told me of an impending railroad catastrophe. A silver and blue train would derail, with lots of injuries as a result. She saw this for late November or early December of that year.

On December 3, the Southern Crescent en route to Washington from the South derailed on a curve near Charlottesville, Virginia, killing six people and injuring forty.

On December 19, 1978, Yolana spoke to me of an airplane crash "over hills or mountains in a suburban area." She felt that there would be trouble with the left wing and that there would be casualties. The figure 7 was also part of her vision. The following day a light plane crashed in a suburban area on the west coast, the left wing hit a tree, and of the seven people aboard, only one survived.

On January 11, 1979, Yolana stated that "one Oriental country would invade another very shortly."

On February 17, China surprised the world by invading Vietnam.

A discotheque in New York City would be struck by a fire, due to candles. The fire occurred in mid-February of 1979.

On January 16, 1979, Yolana spoke of a "terror ride" on a train going to Coney Island.

On February 26, 1979, a holdup man terrorized and victimized people on just such a train.

On December 17, 1978, Yolana told me she foresaw a bombing at a busy New York terminal right after the New Year.

People would be hurt and it would be the work of a crazy person, not political.

On February 19, 1979, three teenagers set fire to a subway token booth, as a result of which three people died. The motive was personal revenge.

On November 15, 1980, Yolana confided to her secretary, Rose Pannini, a vision where she saw someone in terrible danger near black gates. "A man gets out of a car, someone is going to be killed; it is very big—I hear many shots." She thought someone named David was involved. Yolana reported further to this vision, a name like "Lemon" kept running through her mind. Three days later John Lennon was shot in front of the black gates of the Dakota apartments in New York, by a man named Mark David Chapman.

On October 15, 1985, Yolana predicted to me an earthquake near Bernardino, California, that would be felt in New York. This is exactly what happened on February 18, 1986.

At the same time she spoke of a "bombing by the PLO at a military base in Germany" but was not sure about the place name which she thought sounded like "Bogen." As a matter of fact, a nightclub frequented by U.S. personnel was bombed by Arab terrorists. It happened on October 24 in Berlin.

In June of 1994, Yolana gave me the following predictions, prophecies that had come to her unsought during the last year.

An earthquake will hit New York City during the next four years.

A major earthquake will occur in the San Francisco Bay Area during the next two and a half years.

There will be trouble in the Far East involving China and North Korea—and a war in five years.

There will be a nuclear explosion at an upstate New York atomic plant, if the situation is not corrected in time.

A bridge will collapse (George Washington Bridge?) and there will be trouble with the 59th Street Bridge in New York.

Finally, there will be a market crash.

None of these prophecies is particularly new or unique, but coming from Yolana, whose track record with predictions is very good, they need to be noted here.

While not exactly in the same league with Yolana and Rosanna Rogers, a pleasant lady from Brooklyn named Lucy Rivera has over the years proven to me her remarkable gift as a psychic. Although she primarily does private readings, it was startling to me that she came up unexpectedly with spontaneous prophecies.

Lucy visited me on December 27, 1990, very concerned about a vision she had first had during the previous year. In it, she saw four airplanes over Manhattan, which she felt were threatening. She connected this to the then ongoing struggle with Saddam Hussein of Iraq. But she also "saw" a bomb going off and smoke rising in the Wall Street area of Manhattan. The people involved she described wearing a kind of blue uniform like overalls. She saw people running all over and great turmoil. She felt that the people who had caused this came from the Newark, New Jersey, area. The same basic vision recurred to her on January 15, 1991, and then she decided to see me about it so I could warn the authorities, which I did. When the events failed to materialize during the Persian Gulf crisis, I thought no more about it, until the terrible World Trade Center bombing took place two years later. The perpetrators, now jailed for life, did indeed include some that came from New Jersey. The overalls Lucy described in her vision were work clothes the terrorists wore as they were posing as a kind of repair crew when entering the building.

In recent years, Jeane Dixon of Washington, D.C., has become a prophetess of world renown. Ruth Montgomery, a Hearst reporter, has recorded Jeane Dixon's predictions in *A Gift of Prophecy*, which has been a bestseller from the start.

Most famous of Jeane Dixon's prophecies was President Kennedy's assassination, but the coming of Russia's Sputnik and the change in Russia's leadership also rank among her remarkably accurate prophecies, all well documented as to time and circumstances.

Jeane Dixon predicted the fall of Malenkov, the election of President Truman, the death of President Roosevelt, and many other events of lesser political significance. Not all of her predictions have come true, but enough have materialized to secure her a place among the great prophets.

Prophecy, then, is neither to be feared nor ignored. As prophets are human, subject to failure in even the very best of cases, one should consider prophecies as *possibilities* rather than the facts of our future.

Only by acknowledging a higher order governing our destinies can we come to terms with prophecy. But it would be prudent to act as if dire prophecies were to take place as predicted in the sense that we can and must abort them by sheer willpower, spiritual/moral renewal of our lives, and the actions we take in this, our mundane world; for catastrophes involving human beings are the result not only of Divine Will (to test us, perhaps) but very much of human action—for or against, as the case may be. Each prophecy must be dealt with individually, and on its own merits.

Ours is a less than perfect world, and evil is rampant. This evil is expressed by us, the humans. But we also have the power, given us by God, or divine forces if you prefer, to alter the outcome.

About the Author

Hans Holzer is the author of 119 books, including *Life Beyond, The Directory of Psychics, America's Mysterious Places,* and *Window to the Past,* as well as numerous articles for national magazines. He has written, produced, and hosted a number of television programs, most notably "Ghost in the House," "Beyond the Five Senses," and the NBC series "In Search of . . .". He has also appeared as a guest on many national TV shows.

Dr. Holzer, who studied at Vienna University and Columbia University, holds a Ph.D. from the London College of Applied Science. Professor Holzer taught parapsychology for eight years at the New York Institute of Technology. In addition to being a member of the Authors Guild, the Writers Guild of America, the Dramatists' Guild, the New York Academy of Science, and the Archaeological Institute of America, he is listed in *Who's Who in America.* He lives in New York City.